ASK, CONNECT, THRIVE

Unlock Your True Potential- Accelerate Your Career with Mentorship and Networking

JAYA SAI PALETI

ISBN 979-8-89906-942-0

♡ Dedication

<hr>

To my parents,

Mr. Raghavendra Rao Paleti and **Mrs. Manga Devi Paleti**,

whose sacrifices, resilience, and unconditional love have shaped the person I am today.

Without their constant support and hard work, I wouldn't be where I am.

To my family—

My husband, Praneeth Kumar Gadamsetty,

for standing beside me through every chapter of this journey,

and **my daughter, Durga Shanvika,**

whose innocent laughter and presence bring joy and meaning to my days.

And to my silent anchor,

My mother-in-law, Mrs. Nagamani Gadamsetty,

whose quiet yet powerful support helped me manage both my home and my dreams.

This book reflects the love, sacrifices, and unwavering support of all of you.

With love and gratitude—always.

Preface:
Rediscovering Connection in a
Disconnected World

I still remember sitting at my desk on my first day back from maternity leave, staring at my screen, feeling like a stranger in my career. The once-familiar world of deadlines and projects now felt overwhelming. I wasn't just catching up on missed work—I was questioning my place in it.

I hesitated to ask for help, convincing myself, *"I should know this already."* But the truth is, none of us has all the answers—especially during unexpected transitions. It wasn't until I found a community of like-minded individuals that everything changed. They didn't just provide answers—they helped me rediscover my purpose and confidence.

In those moments, I realised a truth that transformed my struggle into clarity: growth doesn't come from knowing everything—it comes from embracing connection, sharing, and learning from others. What began as a personal struggle to regain clarity soon transformed into something bigger—a realisation that many professionals, not just new parents, face similar challenges.

After the COVID-19 pandemic, something subtle but profound changed how we interact. Despite spending more time than ever at work, side by side with colleagues, we hesitate to ask for guidance. The world has become more digital, our screens have become our closest companions, and the people around us have become distant. Our desks hold a laptop—the black box that consumes our focus—and our hands grip a smartphone, a small but powerful device that keeps us connected yet disconnected simultaneously.

But does this mean we should stop reaching out? Should we let go of the human connections that help us grow?

I wrote this book because I believe we shouldn't. Career growth isn't just about learning the latest technology or putting in long hours—it's about the people you interact with, the mentors who guide you, and the relationships you build along the way.

This book is an invitation for you to take charge of your career. To make every human interaction count. To move beyond silent struggles and embrace mentorship, collaboration, and personal growth.

Because success isn't just about what you know—it's about who you connect with and how you choose to grow, day by day, with empathy and humanity.

Let's begin this journey together.

Contents

Introduction

What Do You Do When Google Doesn't Have the Answers? Need a solution? Stack Overflow has your back. But what if the answers you're looking for aren't in the search results? What if you stand at a career crossroads where no algorithm can guide you?

Many of us enter the IT field with endless curiosity, eager to learn and grow. But as responsibilities pile up—the constant rat race of deadlines, meetings, and technical challenges—it's easy to feel stuck. We hesitate to ask for help, fearing others might think we're incompetent or unworthy of our roles. We wonder, "How does someone with this much experience not know the answer?"

But here's the truth: recognising when to ask for help is a strength, not a weakness. It requires courage to admit we don't have all the answers, and humility to seek support when navigating uncharted territory. Asking for help demonstrates self-awareness—a key quality for leadership—and a commitment to growth.

The Power of Asking When Google fails, mentorship shines. Unlike algorithms, mentors provide context, empathy, and insights shaped by their journeys. They can help identify blind spots, encourage self-reflection, and guide us toward solutions that transcend quick fixes.

Even ancient wisdom from texts like the *Mahabharata* emphasises the value of mentorship. This timeless principle—that even the most capable individuals need mentors—is as relevant today as it was thousands of years ago.

Just as Krishna guided Arjuna, the support of mentors can illuminate the path through challenging times. This became clear to me during one of the most uncertain phases of my career.

The Hidden Cost of Isolation in IT Careers

Returning to work after maternity leave felt like stepping into a parallel universe—familiar, yet oddly alien. The confidence I once had seemed out of reach. Doubts clouded my mind, and I found myself asking questions I never thought I'd face:

- Do I still have what it takes?
- Am I falling behind?
- Who do I even ask for guidance?

I considered talking to my manager but wasn't sure if he would understand—or if he would see it as a weakness. I felt overwhelmed, stuck between uncertainty and the fear of asking for help.

A Turning Point Then, as if a ray of light, I reconnected with an old friend. I shared my struggles, and his advice was simple yet powerful: *"Calm down. Take it slow. Look around. Find people. Network. Participate in collaborative events. You'll find clarity."*

That conversation marked a turning point for me. I realised I didn't have to navigate this journey alone. I decided to actively seek mentorship and reached out to an experienced professional I admired. I shared my dilemma: *"Should I pursue leadership or stay in a technical role?"*

Why Technical Skills Alone Aren't Enough

Her response shifted my entire perspective: *"There's no wrong choice. If you want to stay technical, become a subject matter expert. If you want leadership, embrace it. But remember—good leaders don't just manage; they understand the code, the people, and the bigger picture."*

Her words made sense, but then another doubt crept in: *What about AI? With AI taking over, does it even make sense to pursue a technical career?*

That's when she gave me a perspective that completely redefined how I saw my career: *"AI can answer your questions, but it can't solve real-world problems. AI is trained on past data—it predicts, suggests, and automates. But a true subject matter expert understands the end-to-end system, the context behind decisions, and the unforeseen challenges that AI can't predict. AI tools like Chatgpt provide pieces of the puzzle, but only you, armed with experience and expertise, can put it all together."*

The Human Element: This was my breakthrough moment. I realised that no matter how advanced AI becomes, it will always be a tool, not a replacement for human expertise, creativity, and problem-solving. AI can generate data-driven insights, but it takes human intuition and experience to interpret those insights in a meaningful way.

Technical Excellence Meets Leadership Skills: Both paths—technical expertise and leadership—require the ability to navigate complexity, communicate effectively, and anticipate challenges. While technical skills build the foundation, it's soft skills like problem-solving, empathy, and adaptability that elevate careers to new heights.

The Role of AI in Shaping Careers: Instead of fearing AI, we should see it as an enabler. AI can handle repetitive tasks, freeing us to focus on innovation, strategy, and collaboration. It's not about competing with AI; it's about complementing it. Subject matter experts and leaders alike have the unique ability to bring context, creativity, and ethical judgment to decisions that AI cannot fully grasp.

Reflection for Readers Consider this: How can you leverage your technical skills while building the soft skills that make you indispensable in the age of AI? What role do you see yourself playing in shaping the future, where humans and AI work together to solve complex challenges?

How the Right Mentor and Strong Connections Accelerate Career Growth

During COVID-19, when the world shifted to remote work, companies didn't just focus on productivity tools—they invested heavily in collaboration tools like Zoom, Slack, and Microsoft Teams. But why?

If working alone were truly effective, why would companies spend billions ensuring people could connect?

Because collaboration is the lifeline of innovation. The greatest breakthroughs don't happen in isolation; they happen when people talk, share, and build together.

Even ancient texts echo this truth. The *Mahabharata* illustrates how the greatest leaders—whether it's Yudhishthira or Arjuna—thrived with mentors and allies by their side. Similarly, modern industry leaders like Bill Gates, Steve Jobs, Elon Musk, and Sundar Pichai didn't navigate their paths alone. Mentorship and strong networks were their greatest assets, shaping their visions and enabling their successes. If millionaires and visionaries don't Google their way to success, why should we?

The Invitation to Collaborate. As professionals, we must recognise the transformative power of mentorship and connections. Whether you're seeking guidance, offering your expertise, or simply connecting with peers, every conversation has the potential to unlock growth and new opportunities. Collaboration isn't just a tool—it's a mindset, a practice, and a pathway to personal and professional evolution.

What This Book Will Teach You

This book is for every IT professional who has ever felt lost, stuck, or hesitant to seek help. Inside, you'll discover:

- ☑ How to overcome hesitation and ask for guidance
- ☑ Why mentorship accelerates growth faster than self-learning
- ☑ Real-life stories of IT professionals whose careers were transformed through collaboration
- ☑ Ancient wisdom on mentorship from spiritual texts like the Mahabharata
- ☑ Actionable steps to build a strong network and mentorship circle

Your Next Big Break is One Conversation Away. Returning to the workforce or navigating a stagnant career doesn't have to be a solo quest. The smartest professionals know that the right connections can change everything.

This book is your guide to taking that first step—to *Ask, Connect,* and *Thrive.* Together, let's unlock your true potential—one conversation at a time.

Are you ready to take charge of your career? Let's begin. 🚀 "Every journey begins with a single step, and your next step starts here."

Part 1

The Power of Asking for Help

Chapter 1

The Hidden Barrier—Why We Struggle to Ask for Help

Introduction: The Myth of the Lone Genius

The idea of the **"lone genius"** is one of the most persistent myths in IT. From movies about tech prodigies to stories of famous coders who built their careers in garages, we're led to believe that success comes from **pure brilliance and relentless independence**—the developer who locks themselves in a room, churns out code, and emerges with a world-changing solution.

💬 *But here's the truth: No one succeeds alone.*

Behind every major innovation, breakthrough, and successful IT leader is a network of mentors, collaborators, and advisors. They provide guidance, challenge assumptions, and offer perspectives we might never arrive at alone.

Still, many of us hesitate to ask for help. Why?

Think back to school or college, where teachers encouraged us to ask questions if we had doubts and emphasised learning through collaboration with friends. In those environments, curiosity and seeking help were celebrated as vital to growth. Yet, as we enter adulthood and begin professional careers, something changes. We start to lose the art of asking for help, often thinking that needing assistance means we're no longer capable or that we must know everything ourselves.

For some, it's the fear of being judged or seen as incompetent—a fear rooted in the high standards we set for ourselves and the perception that asking for help equates to admitting failure. For others, cultural expectations of self-reliance can discourage seeking support, with phrases like "figure it out yourself" ingrained from an early age. And sometimes, it's simply a matter of pride—believing we must "earn" respect by solving challenges alone.

But the cost of hesitation can be high. Struggling in isolation not only delays solutions but also limits our growth and potential.

This chapter is about breaking that illusion. We'll uncover why technical skills alone aren't enough to grow your career and how collaboration and mentorship are the real game-changers. I'll share personal experiences—moments where I learned these lessons the hard way—and insights from industry leaders who shattered the lone genius myth.

Case Study: The Breakthrough That Took 20 Minutes Instead of Days

Early in my career, I believed that solving problems **alone** was a badge of expertise. I prided myself on being resourceful, convinced that if I just put in **enough effort**, I could tackle **any coding challenge.**

Then one day, I encountered a **bug** that had me stumped. I tried everything—tweaked my code, scoured forums, and reread documentation multiple times. But no matter what I did, the error wouldn't budge. Hours stretched into **days**, and with a **critical deadline looming**, I felt the weight of frustration intensify.

💬 *"What am I missing? Why can't I figure this out?"*

Yet, I hesitated to ask for help. **Would my colleagues think I was incompetent?**

On the **third day**, a senior colleague happened to stop by my desk. Hesitant but desperate, I mentioned the issue. I kept my explanation vague, embarrassed to admit how stuck I was.

But to my surprise, **he didn't judge me**. He asked a few questions, looked at my code, and within **20 minutes**, he pointed out the root cause—a small oversight in how I was handling dependencies.

Three days of frustration, solved in 20 minutes.

The solution felt **embarrassingly simple** in hindsight, but it wasn't that I lacked skills—it was that I was **too deep in my own perspective** to see the issue clearly.

Asking for help isn't just about solving technical challenges. The hesitation can extend to career growth, as I learned in another pivotal moment.

Lesson Learned 💡

- Asking for help doesn't diminish your expertise—it amplifies it.

- Collaboration brings fresh perspectives, unlocking solutions far faster than struggling alone.

The Promotion Struggle: When Technical Skills Weren't Enough

Later in my career, I faced a different challenge. Despite delivering **strong results**, I wasn't being considered for **leadership opportunities**.

💭 *"Isn't my technical expertise enough?"*

Determined to prove myself, I asked my manager for **more responsibilities**. He assigned me **my first project as a team lead**, and I was thrilled. This was my chance to step up. But the excitement didn't last long.

Leadership wasn't just about **doing the work myself**; it was about:

- Coordinating the team
- Delegating tasks
- Fostering collaboration

And I had never practised these skills before.

As an introvert, I hesitated to **delegate**. Instead, I **piled on the workload myself**, convinced I had to prove I could handle it **alone**. And the result is:

- I was **overwhelmed**.
- I was **burned out**.
- I was still **struggling to meet expectations**.

The Game-Changing Advice

One evening, a friend called me. As we talked, I vented my frustrations. My friend listened and then asked:

💬 *"Why are you doing everything alone? Isn't that what your team is for?"*

His words hit me like a **wave of relief**.

For the first time, I realised that **collaboration wasn't a crutch—it was a strength**. I started **observing my team**, identifying their strengths, and assigning tasks based on their unique skills:

- **The detail-oriented member** handled quality assurance.

- **The creative problem-solver** tackled the trickiest technical challenges.

- **The communicator** managed stakeholder updates and team coordination.

The result? The project finished **ahead of schedule**, and the quality exceeded expectations. But the real lesson was this:

Lesson Learned 💡

- Leadership isn't about doing everything yourself—it's about empowering others.

- Great leaders build trust, delegate wisely, and amplify their team's collective potential.

The Google and Stack Overflow Myth

Let's face it—when we encounter a technical challenge, our first instinct is often to Google it or check Stack Overflow. But here's the catch: these tools provide quick fixes, not deep understanding.

I once found a **highly upvoted solution** on Stack Overflow, implemented it confidently, and thought the problem was solved. But during testing, inconsistencies emerged. The fix had only addressed the **symptom**, not the **root cause**.

Had I discussed the issue with **a mentor**, I would have avoided **wasting time and potential rework**.

While platforms like Stack Overflow address immediate technical issues, mentorship cultivates critical thinking, decision-making, and a deeper understanding of challenges, all essential for long-term growth

Lesson Learned 💡

- Google and Stack Overflow are great tools, but they don't replace human insight.

- Mentorship provides context and depth that no algorithm can.

How Top Engineers and Leaders Relied on Mentorship

Still not convinced? Consider this:

- **Steve Jobs** relied on **Bill Campbell**, the "Trillion Dollar Coach," to navigate challenges.

- **Bill Gates** credits **Warren Buffett** for teaching him **strategic thinking**.

- **Elon Musk** collaborates with experts across industries to execute his visions.

These stories remind us that **seeking mentorship isn't a sign of inadequacy—it's a hallmark of greatness.**

Key Takeaways

- The myth of the 'lone genius' is just that—a myth.

- Collaboration accelerates growth. Fresh perspectives unlock solutions faster.

- Technical skills alone aren't enough. Leadership & collaboration set you apart.

- Mentorship matters. The greatest tech leaders had mentors guiding them.

Closing Thought & Call to Action

Success in IT isn't about how much you can do alone—it's about how well you can grow, learn, and collaborate with others.

The decision to seek help can feel daunting, but it's also the most transformative choice you can make for your career.

Looking Ahead: How Mentorship Can Transform Your Career

If mentorship can solve immediate challenges, imagine what it can do for your long-term growth.

So, how do you find a mentor who aligns with your aspirations? That's exactly what we'll explore in the next chapter.

Chapter 2

Google Can't Get You Promoted—But a Mentor Can

Introduction: The Hidden Career Shortcut No One Talks About

Imagine this: You're an ambitious software engineer. You've spent years mastering your craft—writing clean code, learning the latest technologies, and earning certifications. You've burned the midnight oil on countless projects, delivered results, and even taken on leadership responsibilities.

When the next round of promotions is announced, you're confident this is your time. Finally, all your hard work will be recognised.

But as the names are read out, your heart sinks. Your name isn't there.

At first, you're stunned. Then, frustration creeps in. *"What am I missing? What more could I possibly do?"*

Days turn into weeks, and the sting of that missed promotion doesn't fade. Instead, it leads to deeper reflection. You start replaying moments in your career—projects where you excelled, the late nights, the extra effort. The question keeps nagging you: *Why wasn't it enough?*

Doubt begins to surface. *"Did I not push hard enough? Am I not leadership material? Is there something everyone else knows that I don't?"*

It's an invisible ceiling—one that seems impossible to break. But then, you start to notice something. Colleagues who have successfully climbed the ladder weren't just hard workers; they had something more. They had someone guiding them.

And that's when it hits you: *You don't just need more effort. You need the kind of insider knowledge that only comes from experience—experience you don't yet have. What you need is a mentor.*

The Harsh Reality

- Google won't give you a promotion.
- YouTube tutorials won't get you a leadership role.
- Certifications alone aren't enough.

What you need isn't another online course or late-night coding session. **You need insider knowledge**—the kind of insights that aren't in books, forums, or webinars.

The Secret? A Mentor 💡

- A mentor reveals the unwritten rules of career growth.
- A mentor shows you how to navigate office politics.
- A mentor helps you avoid common mistakes and seize opportunities.

A mentor doesn't just teach you to **work harder**—they teach you to **work smarter**.

💡 **Growth Capsule:** *"You can teach yourself to code, but you can't teach yourself experience. That's what a mentor gives you."*

Why Mentorship Matters (With Real Data and Trends)

The power of mentorship isn't just anecdotal—it's backed by research and industry trends. Let's look at the numbers:

Fact	Insight
70% of employees with mentors	They are more likely to receive promotions than those without mentors.
94% of employees	Would stay at a company longer if it invested in its learning and mentorship.
Mentorship boosts retention rates.	Companies with structured mentoring programs see retention rates of 72%, compared to 49% for those without.
Fortune 500 companies	98% of Fortune 500 companies have mentoring programs, and their profits are over 2x higher than companies without mentoring.
Trending on job portals	Platforms like LinkedIn and Naukri now offer mentorship options, recognising their importance in shaping careers.

Why This Matters

These statistics prove that mentorship isn't just a personal boost—it's a game-changer for career growth. The fact that job portals and organisations alike are embracing mentorship highlights a profound realisation: Professionals need more than technical skills to succeed—they need guidance, clarity, and support from those who've walked the path before them.

Seeking mentorship is easier than ever. *With tools and platforms making it simple to connect with potential mentors, and company programs focusing on collaboration, careers can be accelerated through the right relationships. Whether it's asking for advice, building networks, or fostering mentorship, the journey to success begins with reaching out.*

Section 1: The Limits of Self-Learning vs. Guided Learning

As IT professionals, we take pride in being self-learners. * Need to learn Python? There's an online course for that. * Facing a bug? Stack Overflow has your back. * Want career advice? Google "how to get promoted in IT."

Self-learning has given us tremendous independence. But it comes with one critical flaw: it assumes you already know what you need to learn.

- What if your struggle to get promoted isn't about mastering technical skills?

- What if the real problem lies in visibility, influence, or leadership presence?

This is where self-learning hits its limits. It's like trying to fix a car without knowing what's broken. Sure, you might eventually figure it out, but at what cost? Time, energy, and missed opportunities that could have been avoided.

Now imagine this: You've spent months trying to improve your leadership presence by watching online videos, but you're still overlooked during team meetings. You start to feel stuck, unsure if you're making progress. Meanwhile, your colleague, guided by a mentor, receives personalised advice, avoiding rookie mistakes and gaining the attention of senior leadership in half the time.

This is the game-changer that mentorship brings: clarity and direction. A mentor offers guidance that goes far beyond technical skills. They help you spot blind spots, anticipate challenges, and find faster routes to success—areas where self-learning simply can't compete.

💡 Growth Capsule: "Self-learning builds your skills; mentorship builds your future.

Section 2: Why Mentorship is 10x Faster Than Trial & Error

Let me introduce you to two developers:

Developer A (The Self-Learner): Developer A is an incredibly hardworking professional. Every evening after work, he dives into online courses to learn leadership skills. He stays late in the office, hoping his extra efforts will catch someone's attention. Yet, year after year, he watches his peers climb the ladder while he remains stuck. Frustration begins to seep in as he wonders, *"What am I doing wrong? Why doesn't anyone notice my potential?"* He's stuck in the cycle of trial and error, unsure of which step will finally propel him forward.

Developer B (The Mentored Professional): Developer B, on the other hand, took a different approach. Early in his career, he sought out a mentor—a seasoned leader who shared their hard-won lessons. Through regular conversations, his mentor offered actionable feedback, pointing out the importance of visibility and strategic relationships. With this guidance, Developer B avoided common pitfalls and focused on building influence and trust within the team. In just two years, he achieved a promotion, skipping the frustration and uncertainty that Developer A faced.

Who do you think will succeed faster?

💡 Real-World Example:

Satya Nadella, CEO of Microsoft, credits mentorship as the turning point in his career. When Steve Ballmer advised him that leadership and vision, not technical expertise, propel people to the top, Nadella shifted his focus and built strategic relationships that shaped his journey.

Section 3: My Journey—From Struggles to Success in Finding the Right Mentor

Early on in my career, I was eager to find a mentor to help me navigate my challenges. I connected with someone whose work I deeply admired, and for the first few days, things seemed promising. We exchanged ideas, and I felt energised by her insights.

But then things began to shift. Scheduled conversations were missed, and when we did connect, the discussions often felt rushed and distracted. At first, I blamed myself: *Was I asking too much? Was my situation not worth her time?* Frustration turned into self-doubt, and I even questioned whether mentorship was worth the effort. "Maybe mentorship isn't for me," I thought.

The emotional toll was heavier than I expected. I felt stuck, isolated, and disheartened by the mismatch in our goals. But instead of giving up, I took a step back and reflected on what went wrong. That's when I realized the issue wasn't with mentorship itself—it was the lack of alignment. Our paths, while both valuable, simply didn't intersect in a meaningful way.

Determined to try again, I refined my approach. The next time I reached out to someone, I was much more deliberate:

- ☑ I clearly **articulated why I needed a mentor** at this point in my career.

- ☑ I explained **why I specifically chose them** and how their expertise aligned with my goals.

- ☑ I asked for **targeted advice** on my challenges, rather than leaving the conversation open-ended.

This time, it clicked.

This time, it clicked. My mentor, though incredibly busy, felt valued by my thoughtful approach and was eager to help. The guidance I received was transformational, and it shaped my understanding of what mentorship could truly achieve.

Reflecting on this journey, I learned an essential truth: *"These challenges weren't just obstacles—they were invaluable lessons that shaped my understanding of what effective mentorship truly looks like."*

Key Lessons About Mentorship:

- It's not just about finding *any* mentor—it's about finding the **right one** whose expertise aligns with your goals.

- Mentorship works best when you approach it with **clarity, intentionality, and respect** for your mentor's time.

Section 4: Avoiding Common Mentorship Pitfalls

Choosing the wrong mentor can lead to:

- **Frustration:** Spending months seeking advice from a mentor, only to realise their insights didn't align with your leadership challenges. It leaves you feeling stuck, disillusioned, and questioning whether mentorship works at all.

- **Misalignment:** Receiving guidance that feels disconnected from your immediate struggles, making the advice hard to implement or less impactful.

- **Discouragement:** After a bad mentorship experience, many professionals give up entirely, not realising that compatibility is key.

How to Avoid Common Mentorship Mistakes

1. **Be Clear About Your Goals** Before approaching anyone, ask yourself: *Are your aspirations crystal clear, or are they clouded by uncertainty? What specific barriers stand in your way?* o What do I want to achieve in the next 6–12 months? o What specific challenges am I facing right now? o What kind of expertise or perspective do I need to overcome these challenges?

   For example, if your goal is to transition into leadership, look for someone who has successfully made that leap themselves.

2. **Research Potential Mentors** A great mentor isn't just someone you admire—it's someone who aligns with your current needs. Look for: o Senior leaders in your organisation whose careers you'd like to emulate. o Former managers or colleagues who have specific experience in your areas of interest. o Professionals in your network with a proven track record in navigating challenges similar to yours.

3. **Make the First Move—Thoughtfully** Instead of jumping in with "Can you be my mentor?" (which can feel intimidating or vague), craft your ask with specificity: o Start with a compliment: "I admire how you navigated [specific achievement] in your

career." o Follow with context: "I'm currently working on transitioning into leadership and would value your perspective on [specific challenge]." o Ask for a small commitment: "Could we have a 20-minute conversation over coffee to discuss your experience?"

When you're specific about why you're reaching out, potential mentors are more likely to engage and feel excited to share their expertise.

4. **Be Persistent, But Respectful.** Not every mentorship request will lead to a perfect match. Some people may not have the time or bandwidth. That's okay—don't take it personally. Move on to the next potential mentor, and keep refining your approach.

Why The Right Mentor Sticks With You

When you approach mentorship thoughtfully, both you and your mentor benefit:

- **It's a Partnership:** By clarifying your goals and showing respect for their time, mentors feel appreciated and invested in your success.

- **It's Purpose-Driven:** When you choose someone whose expertise aligns with your challenges, their advice resonates deeply and feels actionable.

"A great mentor doesn't just answer your questions—they guide you toward solutions you didn't even know you needed."

💡 *With the right mentor and a thoughtful approach, you're not just building a career—you're shaping a legacy.*

The 90-Day Plan to Thrive in Mentorship

Mentorship thrives on alignment and intentionality.

Now that we've addressed the importance of finding the right mentor and how to avoid common mistakes, let's move into a step-by-step plan to establish and nurture a strong mentorship relationship.

As you embark on this plan, take a moment to think about where you are in your career. What's holding you back? What's your next big milestone? This clarity will help you align your mentorship journey with your unique needs.

📅 Month 1: Identify, Reach Out, and Establish the Connection

This phase is all about finding the right mentor and setting the foundation for a strong relationship.

1. Define Your Goals:

- Identify one or two key challenges you're facing. For example:

  - *I want to improve my leadership presence and visibility in team discussions.*

  - *I'm struggling to manage stakeholder expectations effectively.*

- Be specific about what you hope to achieve through mentorship.

2. Research Potential Mentors:

- Look for someone whose expertise and experience align with your goals. Mentors can include:

  - Senior leaders within your organisation.

- Former colleagues or managers who understand your field.

- Professionals in your broader network with relevant experience.

3. Craft Your Message Thoughtfully:

- Avoid asking directly, *"Can you be my mentor?"* Instead, try:

  - *"I admire your approach to [specific achievement]. Would you be open to a short conversation about [specific challenge]?"*

  - *"I'd love to learn from your experience as I work on [specific goal]. Could we schedule a 20-minute coffee chat?"*

4. First Meeting Goals:

- Introduce yourself and your goals. Share why you've approached them specifically.

- Set the tone for the relationship by emphasising your commitment to learning and growth.

📅 *Month 2: Build Rapport and Start Meaningful Conversations*

Once the mentorship begins, focus on creating a productive dynamic and building trust.

1. Prepare for Every Conversation:

- Come with a clear agenda. Outline specific topics or questions you'd like to discuss. For example:

  - *"I'd like your perspective on how to handle feedback during team meetings."*

  - *"Could you share tips on improving cross-functional collaboration?"*

2. Ask Open-Ended Questions:

- Encourage deeper insights by framing your questions thoughtfully. Instead of *"What should I do?"*, try:

  - *"How did you approach similar challenges in your career?"*

  - *"What would you do differently if you were in my position?"*

3. Address Confidentiality Concerns:

- If you're hesitant to share certain struggles, set expectations early. For example:

  - *"I'd like to discuss some challenges I'm facing, but I want to ensure this stays between us. Is that okay?"*

- Remember, a mentor's role is to guide, not judge. Most mentors respect confidentiality and are invested in your growth.

4. Overcome "Dumb Question" Anxiety

We've all hesitated to ask a question, worrying it might sound "too obvious" or "basic." It's a natural reaction, but here's the good news: mentors appreciate curiosity because it shows your willingness to grow.

💡 **Curiosity Is Celebrated:** Every question, no matter how small, moves you closer to clarity and growth. In mentorship, asking questions is an act of self-advocacy and intentional learning.

One of my mentors once said something that stuck with me:

"There are no dumb questions. Asking is how we grow—and your courage to ask shows your commitment to improvement."

Practical Tips to Build Confidence in Asking Questions

- **Think of It as a Dialogue, Not a Test:**
    - Mentors don't expect you to have all the answers—that's why you're seeking their guidance.
- **Frame Your Questions Positively:** If you feel awkward, try:
    - Instead of: *"I don't understand this—what do I do?"*
    - Say: *"I'd like to better understand this concept. Could you share how you approached it?"*

Why Asking Questions Helps Build Trust

Mentorship is a safe space to clarify doubts, explore challenges, and learn without fear of judgment. When you ask questions, it shows your mentor that you value their experience and are serious about growing.

💡 **Remember:** The only "dumb question" is the one you don't ask. Every question you ask, big or small, is a stepping stone toward clarity, growth, and confidence.

Remember, curiosity isn't a weakness—it's your superpower. Every question you ask demonstrates your drive to learn and grow.

Key Takeaways

- At the end of each meeting, summarise the main points discussed and actionable advice.
    - *For example: "Thanks for sharing your perspective on delegation. My next steps will be to outline roles more clearly with my team."*

📅 Month 3: Apply Advice, Track Progress, and Strengthen the Relationship

The final phase of this plan focuses on taking action, providing updates, and ensuring the mentorship remains impactful.

1. Put Their Advice Into Action:

- Apply one or two pieces of advice from each conversation.

  - *For example, if your mentor suggests delegating more effectively, experiment with assigning tasks based on team members' strengths.*

- Share your progress in future conversations:

  - *"After our last meeting, I tried your suggestion to delegate X task, and it worked well. Thanks for the advice!"*

2. Follow Up with Results:

- Mentors appreciate seeing how their guidance has made a difference. Keep them updated on your achievements:

  - *"I wanted to share that after our discussion on presentation skills, I applied your tips during the quarterly meeting, and it helped me feel more confident."*

3. Expand the Relationship:

- Once trust and rapport are established, explore deeper topics. For example:

  - *"I'd love to hear about pivotal decisions in your career— what influenced them, and what lessons did you learn?"*

4. Express Gratitude:

- A simple "thank you" goes a long way. Recognise their time and effort:

  - *I'm so grateful for your insights—they've already helped me approach challenges differently.*

By the end of these 90 days, you won't just have a mentor—you'll have a partnership that fuels your professional growth. Mentorship is a journey, and this is only the beginning of what you can achieve together.

From Connection to Confidence: How a 90-Day Mentorship Plan Unlocks Your Leadership Potential:

Month 1: Identify, Reach Out, and Establish the Connection

Meet Meena, a mid-level manager. She often finds herself wondering whether climbing the ladder as a woman in leadership is truly achievable. She's faced with societal stereotypes, internal doubts, and the belief that leadership roles demand far more time and energy than she can manage.

One day, she notices a senior manager—a woman—who has successfully established herself in a high-level position. Meena begins to rethink her assumptions: *"If she's there, why can't I? What am I missing to level up my career?"*

Determined to take control of her growth, Meena embarks on a journey of self-awareness. She starts by evaluating her strengths and identifying areas where she struggles, like managing stakeholder expectations and improving her executive presence. She seeks feedback from trusted colleagues and managers, drafting a clear list of competencies she needs to work on.

Using this newfound clarity, Meena researches potential mentors and zeroes in on the senior manager who inspired her. Crafting a thoughtful message, she writes: *"I admire your leadership style and the way you've successfully navigated into executive roles. As someone working on similar growth areas, I'd love to hear about your journey and seek your advice on managing visibility and influence. Would you be open to a short coffee chat?"*

This approach resonates with her chosen mentor, and they set up a meeting to discuss Meena's goals and challenges, laying the foundation for their mentorship journey.

📅 Month 2: Build Rapport and Start Meaningful Conversations

Now that Meena's mentorship has started, she prepares for every conversation with intentionality. For their second meeting, she shares her agenda in advance: *"I'd love to get your insights on improving collaboration with cross-functional teams, as I've found that alignment often gets lost in translation during projects."*

During their conversation, Meena asks open-ended questions to gain deeper insights, like: *"What strategies worked for you when handling cross-functional misalignment? Are there any mistakes you learned from that I should avoid?"*

Her mentor shares practical advice and even recounts a story of a cross-functional project that taught her the value of clear communication and setting shared goals. Inspired, Meena applies these strategies in her next team meeting and sees immediate results—team members align more effectively, and projects progress smoothly.

This breakthrough not only boosts Meena's confidence but also strengthens the trust between her and her mentor.

📅 Month 3: Apply Advice, Track Progress, and Strengthen the Relationship

Let's now shift to Meena, a mid-level manager seeking to improve his leadership skills. Meena's mentor had advised her to experiment with delegation as a way to build trust and empower his team.

Taking the advice to heart, Meena assigns a critical project task to one of her team members, aligning it with their strengths.

When the task is executed flawlessly, Meena makes sure to credit his colleague during a leadership meeting. This move not only builds rapport within his team but also demonstrates Meena's growing leadership abilities to senior managers.

In her next conversation with her mentor, Meena shares: *"Your advice on delegation has been a game-changer. Not only did my team member exceed expectations, but they also freed me up to focus on strategic priorities. Thank you for guiding me through this!"*

This exchange deepens their mentor-mentee bond, as Meena's mentor feels gratified to see the tangible impact of their guidance.

Having completed the 90-day plan, Meena is now more confident in her leadership abilities. Her cross-functional collaboration has improved, and she's successfully implemented her mentor's advice on managing stakeholder expectations. But she knows mentorship isn't a "one-and-done" process—it's an ongoing journey of growth.

In one of her follow-up conversations, Meena shares an exciting development: *"Your advice about creating clear action plans for team discussions has not only made me more confident but also impressed our director. She even hinted that I should prepare for a stretch project—something I've always wanted!"*

Her mentor responds with encouragement but also challenges Meena to think bigger: *"That's a great step forward, but let's consider what this stretch project could mean for your long-term goals. How can you position yourself as someone ready for even more strategic responsibilities?"*

Inspired, Meena outlines a six-month personal development plan, focusing on cultivating executive presence. She requests her mentor's guidance on presenting her ideas persuasively to senior leaders. Together, they simulate scenarios where Meena must pitch innovative solutions to leadership, receiving real-time feedback to sharpen her skills.

As Meena grows more adept at strategic communication, she begins mentoring junior colleagues on topics like managing visibility and influence. This mentorship dynamic becomes a two-way street—Meena gains leadership experience while paying forward the guidance she's received.

She learns that Mentorship isn't just about receiving career advice—it's about unlocking opportunities, accelerating growth, and gaining insights that self-learning alone can't provide. When approached with intentionality, mentorship can be the single most powerful lever in your career progression.

Key Takeaways

- **Mentorship is transformational:** It bridges the gap between hard work and impactful career growth by guiding visibility, leadership, and navigating challenges.

- **Clarity is crucial:** Clearly define your goals and challenges before seeking a mentor to ensure alignment and maximise impact.

- **Intentionality builds success:** Thoughtful outreach, consistent follow-ups, and actionable steps strengthen the mentor-mentee relationship and drive meaningful results.

- **Growth is a two-way street:** Mentorship is a journey— adapt the relationship as your goals evolve, and pay it forward by mentoring others.

❋ Pro Tips for Mentor-Mentee Conversations

1. **Be Transparent About Your Concerns:**

   - If discussing sensitive challenges, set clear boundaries early.

   - For example: *"I want to share a challenge I'm navigating at work, but I'd like to keep this discussion private."*

2. **Normalise Asking Questions:**

   - Don't hesitate to ask—even seemingly simple questions show active learning and reflection.

   - Mentors appreciate curiosity; it's a sign of genuine engagement.

3. **Be Open to Feedback:**

   - Sometimes, a mentor's advice might challenge your perspective—embrace it as a chance for growth and self-improvement.

4. **Prepare and Respect Their Time:**

   - Be punctual and come to meetings prepared with specific topics or questions. Respect their busy schedule by making the most of your time together.

◇ **Final Thought: Unlocking Your Next Step** "Mentorship has the potential to transform your career. Whether you're identifying a mentor, preparing thoughtful questions, or taking the first leap toward building a connection, one small step today can open doors to opportunities you never imagined."

◎ Your Challenge for the Week

1. Identify one key career challenge you're currently facing (e.g., "I want to improve my executive presence.").

2. Pinpoint one potential mentor who has the expertise to guide you through this challenge.

3. Draft a personalised, concise message inviting them to connect and have a conversation.

💡 *Every mentorship journey begins with a single conversation. Take that step today and start building the career you deserve.* 🚀

Chapter 3

The Networking Myth—Why You're Doing It Wrong

Introduction: The Illusion of Networking

In today's professional world, networking is often viewed as the golden key to career mobility. The mantra is everywhere: *"Your network is your net worth."* But for many, despite attending countless networking events, sending LinkedIn requests, and collecting business cards, the question remains: *Why hasn't this unlocked meaningful opportunities?*

People often believe that attending networking events will instantly open doors. But in reality, networking is more nuanced. From my own experience, I've seen professionals approach these events in very different ways—and not all lead to success:

- Some recognise familiar faces but hesitate to interact, missing the chance to form meaningful connections.

- Others dive in, talking to everyone, but leave without remembering the people they met.

- Some show up only to contribute to a specific task, with no desire to maintain a lasting relationship.

- And then some people attend events solely to showcase their presence, hoping to boost visibility within their team or organisation.

Each of these approaches reflects the **intention** behind the effort. If your goal is simply to check a box or boost your image, the true benefits of networking will likely remain out of reach.

Here's the reality:

✔ Collecting contacts ≠ building trust.

✔ Shallow interactions rarely lead to long-term success.

✔ Real networking is about forming genuine, meaningful relationships—not just increasing your numbers.

💡 **Key Takeaway:** *"Real networking is a marathon, not a sprint—it's about deep, meaningful relationships, not just a list of names."*

Networking is often hailed as the ultimate career accelerator, yet so many professionals feel stuck, wondering why it doesn't work as expected. This chapter dives into exactly why traditional approaches fail—and, more importantly, how you can transform your networking efforts into meaningful, career-changing connections.

Why "Networking Events" Aren't Enough

Networking events are meant to provide a space where professionals can ask questions, connect authentically, and build collaborative relationships. In theory, they sound ideal—places brimming with opportunities to form meaningful connections and advance your career.

But here is the problem: these events often fall short in practice. The structure of most networking events rarely allows for deep engagement. You're surrounded by a sea of unfamiliar faces, conversations feel rushed, and the focus shifts from building trust to simply collecting contact information.

From my own experience, I have seen how this plays out: At one event, I noticed several colleagues who were busy trying to talk to *as many people as possible.* They'd exchange a flurry of business cards, but once the event ended, they barely remembered the names or faces. On the flip side, others were hesitant to interact, lingering around familiar faces and missing the opportunity to expand their network altogether.

These approaches highlight why networking events alone aren't enough:

- **Limited Time for Authenticity:** Conversations are often superficial due to the event's fast-paced structure.

- **Focus on Numbers, Not Quality:** When the goal is to network with *everyone,* meaningful connections get lost in the rush.

- **Transactional Intentions:** Many attendees prioritise showcasing their participation over fostering real collaboration or mutual growth.

When networking events lack intentionality, they often lead to fleeting interactions instead of lasting relationships. However, with the right mindset, you can shift the dynamic:

- **Connect Authentically:** Prioritise conversations that spark innovation and trust over surface-level exchanges.

- **Collaborate Across Teams:** Use the diversity of attendees to gain fresh perspectives and solve problems creatively.

- **Foster Mutual Growth:** Build relationships based on shared values and long-term goals.

💡 **Key Takeaway:** *"Networking events aren't inherently the problem—it's the intention behind how you approach them. When you attend with genuine intent, you unlock opportunities far beyond mere attendance."*

The PayPal Mafia Effect

How Real Relationships Fuel Success

The story of the PayPal Mafia is a testament to the extraordinary power of authentic, collaborative relationships. This group of early PayPal employees—including icons like Elon Musk, Reid Hoffman, and Peter Thiel—didn't just work together; they forged bonds that reshaped entire industries. Long after their time at PayPal, they went on to create companies that have revolutionised the way we live and work, including Tesla, LinkedIn, YouTube, and Spacex.

What made their connections so remarkable?

- **Shared Struggles and Growth:** At PayPal, they tackled complex challenges under intense pressure, which cultivated trust, respect, and camaraderie.

- **A Foundation of Trust:** Their relationships endured beyond PayPal because they supported one another's ventures, invested in each other's ideas, and shared advice freely.

- **Alignment of Vision:** Their collective passion for innovation and disruption united them, turning their collaborations into enduring alliances.

The PayPal Mafia teaches us a valuable lesson: **success isn't just about individual effort; it's about building authentic relationships that amplify your impact.** When you work with people who share your values, vision, and ambition, you create partnerships that last and multiply opportunities.

💡 **Key Takeaway:** *"True success comes from deep, collaborative relationships that extend beyond professional transactions. When you grow together, those connections become the foundation for innovation and long-term success."*

The Art of Giving Before Asking

Imagine this: you receive a LinkedIn request from someone you barely know, and their very first message is a direct favour request. How does it feel? Chances are, it comes across as transactional and impersonal. Unfortunately, this is a common mistake many professionals make—they ask for something too soon, without first establishing trust or offering value.

So, how can you stand out and build meaningful relationships instead? By flipping the script and focusing on **giving before asking**. Offering value upfront creates trust, fosters goodwill, and lays the foundation for a mutually beneficial connection.

Simple Ways to Offer Value

- **Share Insights:** Highlight an article, resource, or insight that aligns with their interests or work.

- **Compliment Their Work:** Acknowledge their expertise or recent achievements genuinely.

- **Ask Thoughtful Questions:** Spark engaging conversations by showing curiosity and interest in their experiences.

The Principle of Reciprocity

- People are naturally more inclined to help when they feel valued or have already received something meaningful from you.

- Offering assistance, advice, or useful information creates a sense of trust and sets the stage for a lasting relationship.

Real-World Examples

- **Contributing to Open-Source Projects:** IT professionals who make meaningful contributions often find these efforts open doors to mentorship, collaborations, and unexpected opportunities.

- **Engaging Online Thoughtfully:** A well-crafted comment on a blog post, LinkedIn update, or GitHub issue can spark conversations that lead to professional connections or even new opportunities.

💡 **Key Takeaway:** *"Give first, and the ask will come naturally—meaningful relationships are built on mutual benefit, not one-sided requests."*

Building Your Trusted Circle

Who Do You Rely On?

Networking isn't always about expanding your contact list—it's about deepening the connections you already have.

I once faced a personal challenge that brought this truth into sharp focus. Despite having hundreds of contacts saved on my phone—colleagues, acquaintances, and professionals I'd connected with over time—I found myself unsure of who I could truly rely on outside of my family.

This realisation was humbling. It taught me an important lesson: the size of your network matters far less than the depth of your connections. Through a readers' community, I learned to approach networking differently:

Start Small: Reach out to one person you trust and focus on nurturing that relationship first.

Build Consistency: Call someone every day—or if that feels overwhelming, start with one person each week or month.

Focus on Meaningful Interactions: Share your thoughts, seek advice, and genuinely invest in the relationship over time.

By practising this, I discovered:

- Which contacts were reliable for specific challenges?

- How to seek meaningful advice and open up about the issues that truly matter.

- The incredible power of consistency in transforming casual relationships into a trusted network.

Often, the most valuable connections are already within your reach. It's not about how many people you know—it's about nurturing the right relationships and being intentional in your efforts to deepen them.

💡 **Key Takeaway:** *"Sometimes, the most valuable connections are already in your phone. Regularly reaching out builds a trusted network that becomes a lifeline."*

The Unexpected Power of Tea Breaks

A Space for Open Conversations

Networking isn't just about formal meetings or structured events—it's often about the moments in between.

Some of the most insightful work conversations don't happen in boardrooms or scheduled meetings. Instead, they emerge spontaneously, during tea breaks, coffee chats, or hallway conversations. In IT teams, especially, breakthroughs often occur in these informal settings. A casual chat can spark fresh ideas, solve a tricky problem, or deepen your understanding of a colleague's perspective—all in an unstructured, relaxed environment.

While some dismiss tea breaks as downtime or a distraction, they're much more than that. These moments create an opportunity to relieve stress, collaborate naturally, and form authentic connections. They're where relationships grow, ideas flow freely, and innovation thrives.

Think about it

- How often do you gain a new perspective or insight from a casual chat compared to a formal meeting?

- Have you ever solved a complex issue by discussing it over coffee with a colleague?

- Are there team members you rarely talk to but could learn from if you reached out during these moments?

These seemingly small interactions have big potential. It's not just about what *you take* from a conversation—it's about *what you contribute.* Simple gestures, like sharing a resource, offering a fresh perspective, or simply being present and listening, can leave a lasting impact.

Reflective Prompt: Who in your team could you connect with more during tea breaks? What small question or topic could you bring up to spark a meaningful, open conversation this week?

💡 **Key Insight:** *The best networkers focus on adding value first, rather than approaching interactions with a "What can I get?" mindset. Even the simplest acts of collaboration or support during informal moments can create lasting relationships.*

◇ Actionable Strategies to Network the Right Way

Meaningful networking doesn't happen by accident—it requires intentional effort and genuine interactions. Here are practical strategies to build impactful relationships:

Strategy	How to Implement It
Be a Connector	Facilitate introductions between two people in your network who could benefit from collaborating.
Engage Online	Share thoughtful comments on LinkedIn, GitHub, or other platforms. Post content that sparks ideas and conversations.
Join or Create Communities	Get involved with professional groups—online or offline—that align with your interests. If you spot a gap in your industry, consider creating a new community.
Collaborate on Projects	Participate in hackathons, open-source initiatives, or side projects to work with like-minded individuals.
Follow Up Consistently	Reconnect periodically with your contacts by sending a message to check in and maintain the relationship.
Express Gratitude	Show appreciation by thanking someone who helped you, and offer your support to someone else in return.

💡 **Key Insight:** *Each step is a simple, deliberate action that can turn fleeting interactions into lasting connections.*

Small Acts of Contribution

Sharing Your Learnings

Sometimes, even small contributions can have a profound impact. By sharing your knowledge and gratitude, you create value for others while strengthening your network:

- **Share Something New:** Whether it's a fresh idea, recent lesson, or a useful resource, offering knowledge—even if it doesn't solve an immediate problem—leaves a positive impression.

- **Explain Insights to Others:** When you articulate what you've learned to colleagues or peers, you deepen your understanding and inspire growth in those around you.

💡 **Key Takeaway:** *"Consistent, meaningful engagement—coupled with genuine gratitude and small acts of contribution—transforms fleeting interactions into lifelong connections."*

Conclusion: Networking as a Long-Term Investment

- **Networking is a Marathon:** Building genuine relationships takes time, persistence, and a commitment to giving more than you take. It's a journey of sustained effort, not a quick fix.

- **The Compounding Effect:** Each meaningful connection can unlock doors to countless opportunities. As your network deepens, the benefits multiply, creating career growth, collaborations, and mutual success over time.

Your Challenge for the Week

Take small, actionable steps to cultivate your network meaningfully:

1. **Identify Three Professionals:** Choose three people in your field whose work you admire.

2. **Start a Conversation:** Reach out with a thoughtful message—compliment their work or share a relevant insight—but don't ask for a favour right away.

3. **Join a Community:** Engage in a professional group that aligns with your interests. Participate actively to contribute and connect.

4. **Express Gratitude:** Reconnect with someone who has helped you in the past. Thank them, and offer your support to someone else.

5. **Share Your Learnings:** Take a recent insight or lesson you've gained and share it with your team or community.

💡 **Final Thought:** *"True networking is about nurturing relationships, creating mutual value, and leaving a positive impact. When you give genuinely, engage authentically, and express gratitude—no matter how small the gesture—opportunities will follow."*

Chapter 4

The Ask That Changed Everything—Real Stories of IT Growth

Introduction: The Fear of Asking

You're in a team meeting. A complex problem is on the table, and you know your question could bring clarity or even spark a breakthrough. But doubt sets in—*What if I sound inexperienced?* You glance around, hoping someone else will ask the same question. They don't. You stay silent. The moment passes.

How many opportunities have slipped by because you hesitated to ask?

This hesitation is all too common in IT. We work in a field that glorifies self-reliance, where solving problems independently is often seen as a badge of honour. On top of that, impostor syndrome feeds into the fear, whispering that asking for help will expose your shortcomings. The result? Questions left unasked, connections left unexplored, and growth opportunities missed.

But here's the truth: The act of asking isn't a sign of weakness; it's a sign of strength. Courage begins the moment you decide to raise your hand.

💡 **Key Takeaway:** *"The biggest breakthroughs in your career often begin with a simple, courageous ask."*

Why Asking for Help Feels So Hard

The fear of asking stems from a blend of workplace culture, pride, and self-doubt. In the IT industry, where problem-solving is one of the most celebrated skills, asking for help can feel like admitting defeat.

But this mindset couldn't be further from the truth. Consider this: the most successful teams are built on collaboration and the free flow of ideas. It's through asking questions and seeking guidance that innovation thrives.

What holds us back from asking for help?

- **Cultural Pressure:** IT professionals often feel expected to solve problems independently, reinforcing a culture where seeking help is stigmatised.

- **Fear of Judgment:** Many of us worry that asking questions will make us seem less competent or knowledgeable.

- **Overestimating Self-Reliance:** The belief that "I should figure this out myself" often leads to unnecessary roadblocks.

The Solution: Asking for help is a skill—one that grows with practice. By reframing help-seeking as a collaborative act, you transform it into a strength rather than a vulnerability.

💡 **Key Takeaway:** *"Asking for help doesn't make you less capable; it makes you more collaborative and resourceful."*

My Struggle

How Asking Changed Everything

In the early years of my career, communication felt like an insurmountable hurdle. I often hesitated to voice my doubts or ask questions during demos, design calls, or brainstorming sessions. An inner voice whispered fears I couldn't shake:

- *What if my idea doesn't work?*

- *What if they think I'm not smart enough?*

- *What if I embarrass myself in front of my team?*

For a time, my silence blended into the background. As a junior professional, it was easy to dismiss my lack of participation as part of the learning curve. But as I gained experience, the stakes rose—and so did the expectations. My managers noticed my reluctance to engage, and it began to reflect in my performance reviews. I felt increasingly stuck, weighed down by self-doubt.

Determined to break free, I decided to take action. My first attempt was to join Toastmasters, hoping it would help me build confidence and improve my public speaking. Yet, balancing work pressures with regular attendance proved difficult. Progress felt slow, and frustration mounted as the feedback on my communication skills remained unchanged. I felt trapped, unsure of how to move forward—but not ready to give up.

Recognising the need for change, I made a bold decision—I approached my manager. Sharing my struggles felt challenging, but I was determined to be honest. I candidly explained my difficulties balancing work with Toastmasters and emphasised my commitment to personal growth.

That conversation became a turning point. My simple *Ask* for help brought unexpected support and encouragement. Instead of judgment, my manager acknowledged my honesty and dedication, offering practical advice that helped me focus on incremental progress.

With my manager's support, I committed to attending Toastmasters more consistently. Along the way, I found a mentor whose guidance became invaluable. His advice was simple yet profound: *"Even if the sessions are weekly, take small, consistent steps every day. Write a short story daily and share it with me. We'll connect and work on improvements together."*

At first, I doubted myself. I frequently asked questions I feared might seem "dumb," like, *"How can a small adjustment in communication completely change the tone of a meeting?"* But with my mentor's patience and encouragement, I began to see these moments of doubt as opportunities for growth. Slowly but surely, my confidence grew.

The results were undeniable. I became more engaged and proactive in my team, which improved my visibility and performance ratings. Eventually, my efforts led to a well-deserved promotion. Yet the outcomes went beyond professional success—the bond I built with my mentor and the lessons learned from my manager remain among the most valuable aspects of my journey.

Reflecting on this experience, I realise how often professionals hesitate to have such candid conversations with their managers. Fear of judgment or failure can hold them back, yet these discussions have the power to transform careers. For me, that single *Ask* became a bridge to growth, showing that vulnerability is not a weakness but a strength.

💡 **Key Takeaway:** *"The simple act of asking for help can create life-changing opportunities. Don't let fear hold you back—your transformation begins with that first step."*

Real Stories of IT Professionals Who Asked—and Changed Their Careers

Just like my journey, these IT professionals discovered how one simple ask could change everything:

Story 1: The Junior Engineer Who Found a Game-Changing Mentor Akash, a fresh IT graduate, felt overwhelmed by the demands of his first job. Hesitant to ask for help, he struggled to meet expectations. When he finally reached out to Ravi, a senior engineer, he discovered a mentor who believed in his potential.

- **The Stakes:** Without help, Akash risked falling behind and losing confidence.

- **Outcome:** With Ravi's guidance, Akash quickly improved, earned leadership recognition, and eventually became a tech lead.

Story 2: The Mid-Career Professional Who Broke Through a Career Plateau Neha, a mid-career professional, felt stuck despite her hard work. Realising she needed a fresh perspective, she asked a senior leader, *"What do I need to do differently to grow?"* The candid feedback and mentorship she received transformed her career trajectory.

- **The Stakes:** Career stagnation had eroded Neha's confidence.

- **Outcome:** By focusing on high-impact projects, she expanded her influence and earned a promotion.

What unites these stories is the courage to ask. A single question can open doors, spark growth, and lead to life-changing opportunities.

Overcoming Fear & Imposter Syndrome When Asking for Help

The fear of asking often stems from imposter syndrome—the belief that we aren't good enough. But every time you hesitate, remind yourself: even the most successful people started as beginners.

Mindset Shifts

- *From hesitation → to courage*
- *From fear of judgment → to a focus on growth*
- *From "I should know this" → to "How can I learn this?"*

💡 **Key Insight:** *"Asking for help isn't a sign of weakness—it's a sign of wisdom."*

Conclusion: The Power of One Ask

Imagine how your career could transform if you ask, without fear or hesitation, for guidance that unlocks your next step forward. Courage, coupled with small, consistent efforts, can lead to extraordinary outcomes.

Your Challenge for the Week:

1. Identify someone in your field whose expertise could help you.
2. Reach out with a thoughtful question.
3. Reflect on what you learned and how you'll apply it.
4. Build the relationship over time and pay it forward by helping someone else.

Final Thought: *"The growth journey begins with the courage to ask."*

Part 2

The Art of Building Meaningful Connections

Chapter 5

Finding Your Circle—Building a Support System in IT

1. Why IT Professionals Need a Support System

Have you ever felt stuck in your career? Like you are doing all the right things—learning new skills, working late nights, solving tough problems—yet something still feels missing? Maybe you are unsure about your next move, or you see others progressing faster while you struggle alone.

The truth is, you don't have to figure everything out by yourself.

Many IT professionals fall into the "Lone Wolf" trap, believing that career success is purely an individual effort. But if you look at the most successful people in tech—CEOS, top engineers, industry leaders—you'll notice one thing: they all had support systems.

- A mentor who guided them through career-defining moments.
- A peer who challenged them to grow.
- A sponsor who spoke their name in leadership meetings.

In an industry that moves at lightning speed, having the right people around you isn't just helpful—it's essential. The right connections can accelerate your growth, provide clarity in difficult decisions, and open doors to opportunities you never imagined.

Recognising the need for a support system is just the beginning. The next step is identifying the *right people* who can play critical roles in your career journey.

2. Who Should Be in Your Circle?

To thrive in IT, you need more than just colleagues—you need a deliberate support system that includes:

- **The Career Guide (Mentor)** – A senior professional who provides long-term career insights, helping you navigate big decisions. *Example:* As mentioned in the introduction, my mentor guided me during a critical career crossroads. When I was uncertain about pursuing a leadership role or continuing in a technical path, she shared her own experiences, provided clarity on the long-term implications of each choice, and helped me evaluate which aligned best with my strengths and aspirations. Her guidance not only eased my doubts but also gave me actionable steps to move forward with confidence.

- **The Peer Collaborator** – Someone at your level who shares knowledge, helps solve challenges, and grows with you. *Example:* A peer collaborator might have helped you debug a critical issue in an important release, sparking a conversation that led to shared learning and a better solution than either of you could have developed alone.

- **The Sponsor/Advocate** – A leader or manager who actively vouches for you in key discussions about promotions, opportunities, and leadership roles. *Example:* Picture a sponsor who spoke up for you during a leadership meeting, advocating for your promotion and highlighting your achievements, even when you weren't in the room.

- **The Technical Sounding Board** – A go-to person for brainstorming technical problems, discussing industry trends, and keeping up with new developments. *Example:* A technical sounding board might have helped you refine a complex architectural design, offering critical feedback that saved time and improved performance.

- **The Growth Challenger** – Someone who pushes you out of your comfort zone, encouraging you to take on challenges you might hesitate to face alone. *Example: One of my teammates once noticed my ability to handle a task that wasn't formally assigned to me. They urged me to take it up, believing I could excel. Their encouragement not only helped me grow but also demonstrated how a Growth Challenger sees your potential and inspires you to rise to the occasion.*

Key Insight: No one person can play all these roles—your support system should be diverse, covering different aspects of your career.

These examples can help your readers visualise each role and its value in a real-world IT career context. Let me know if you'd like further refinements!

Understanding the roles within your support system is the foundation. The next step is actively seeking out these connections—being deliberate about where and how to find the right people.

3. Where and How to Find Your Circle?

Building a strong support system doesn't happen by accident—you need to be intentional. Here's where to look:

Inside Your Company

- **Mentorship Programs** – Many companies have internal mentorship initiatives—take advantage of them.
- **Leadership Groups** – Engaging with senior leaders can help you gain career sponsorship.
- **Cross-Team Collaborations** – Working on projects with different teams expands your connections.

Industry Communities

- **Conferences & Meetups** – Attending (or speaking at) industry events is a great way to meet like-minded professionals.
- **Open-Source Projects** – Contributing to open-source communities allows you to connect with experts in your field.

LinkedIn & Online Groups

- **Engage Beyond Just Connecting** – Commenting on posts, sharing insights, and starting discussions helps build meaningful relationships.
- **Find Niche Communities** – Instead of generic networking, join groups specific to your interests (e.g., AI, DevOps, Product Management).

Volunteering & Side Projects

- **Tech Nonprofits & Hackathons** – Contributing to meaningful projects can introduce you to passionate professionals.

- **Mentorship Platforms** – Platforms like ADPList, MentorCruise, or local mentorship programs connect you with experienced mentors.

Key Insight: The best connections don't come from random networking—they come from shared experiences and collaboration.

If networking feels overwhelming, start with small, manageable steps. Focus on building one meaningful connection at a time— one thoughtful conversation can lay the foundation for a powerful support system.

4. Building Strong, Meaningful Connections

Making connections is just the first step. Maintaining and strengthening them is where the real value comes in.

- **Giving Before Asking** – Instead of reaching out only when you need something, offer value first (e.g., sharing knowledge, helping with a project, making an introduction).

- **Consistency Matters** – Small, regular check-ins (even a quick "How's everything going?" message) keep relationships strong over time.

- **Being the Connector** – Take one step today by introducing two people in your network—it builds credibility and strengthens your role in the industry.

Remember, the strongest connections thrive on collaboration, trust, and mutual growth—investing in these relationships builds a foundation for long-term success.

5. Action Steps: Strengthening Your Circle Today

Put this into action right now!

- Identify one person who could be a mentor, peer, or advocate.

- Reach out with a thoughtful message or question.

- Join a new group or community to expand your connections.

- Set a monthly check-in reminder to nurture key relationships.

Final Thought

Success in IT isn't just about your technical skills—it's about the people you surround yourself with. *Your support system can be the difference between stagnation and career acceleration.*

Summary

- A strong support system is essential for long-term career growth.

- Your circle should include mentors, peers, advocates, and challengers.

- Great connections come from collaboration, not just networking.

- Consistency and giving value are key to building long-lasting relationships.

- Start strengthening your circle today with simple action steps!

Chapter 6

Debugging Your Career—Identifying and Fixing Bottlenecks

Introduction: Is Your Career Running on an Outdated Version?

Picture your favourite app stuck on a ten-year-old version. It's slow, clunky, and incompatible with today's tools. That's what happens when careers go unmaintained—only the bugs aren't in the code, they're in your skills, mindset, and growth plan.

Think about software updates. Every application gets version upgrades—fixing bugs, improving performance, and adding new features. Yet, when it comes to careers, many professionals keep running on Version 1.0 for years, refusing to upgrade their skills, mindset, or goals.

Here's the truth: Your career needs regular version upgrades—not just debugging—to stay relevant and avoid stagnation.

In this chapter, you'll learn how to:

- Recognise career stagnation before it's too late

- Identify common career bottlenecks that slow down growth

- Leverage mentorship to uncover blind spots
- Implement a 30-Day Career Fix Plan to get unstuck

1. The Mindset Bug—Fixed vs. Growth Mindset

Ever worked with someone who believed they knew everything and never accepted feedback? And then there's the opposite—the ones always learning, adapting, and growing? That's the difference between a **Fixed Mindset** and a **Growth Mindset.**

Fixed Mindset vs. Growth Mindset in Tech

Fixed Mindset (Career Bottleneck Ahead!)	Growth Mindset (Career Acceleration!)
"I'm too old to learn a new language like Rust."	"Learning Rust could open new doors—let me give it a shot!"
"I've been coding in Java for 10 years. I don't need new tech."	"I love Java, but let me explore how AI and cloud tech are evolving!"
"If I ask for help, people will think I'm dumb."	"Asking for help is how I grow and level up."
"I failed at that project, so I'm not good enough."	"I failed? Great—what can I learn from this experience?"

Reflective Call to Action

What mindset bugs are slowing you down? Are you embracing new challenges, or staying in your comfort zone because it feels safe? Take a moment to identify one area in your life where you could shift from a fixed mindset to a growth mindset—and think about a small action you could take today to challenge that limitation.

An Inspiring Example: Overcoming a Fixed Mindset

One of my friends was an incredibly dependable professional, always taking ownership and accountability for tasks assigned to her. However, she was averse to risk and believed that improving her skills wasn't necessary. Her reasoning? "I'm receiving good pay; why should I spend time and energy improving myself when I already have so many responsibilities at home?" Even when she received constructive feedback, she would view it negatively, feeling bad or sad for a few days, but eventually returning to the same habits.

She forgot one crucial fact: especially in IT, continuous learning is essential, and *change is the only constant.*

Years passed, and her fixed mindset started affecting her personal life. When she needed additional income due to financial pressures, she found herself stuck. She couldn't approach her manager for a raise because she knew the feedback she had ignored would come back to haunt her. This was her turning point—a moment of realisation. She finally acknowledged how her fixed mindset had held her back, both professionally and personally.

Determined to change, she took smaller steps to rebuild her career. She enrolled in a certification course, completed it successfully, and began seeking new opportunities to grow instead of staying stagnant. Her journey highlights the power of reflection and how a shift in mindset can open new doors.

Psychological Fact

Neuroplasticity (your brain's ability to rewire and adapt) proves that ANYONE can develop new skills at any stage of their career. The only thing stopping you? Your mindset.

Key Insight: Growth begins at the edge of your comfort zone.

Adopting a growth mindset is the first step, but it's equally important to evaluate whether your current trajectory is truly fostering growth or holding you back. Let's explore how to recognise signs of career stagnation before it's too late.

2. Recognising Career Stagnation Before It's Too Late

Many professionals mistake stagnation for stability. They assume they're "safe"—until layoffs happen, technology shifts, or they realise they've been stuck in the same cycle for years.

Signs You Need a Career Version Upgrade

- **Honest Self-Reflection:** Why are you doing this job? Is it just for the paycheck, or are you truly growing and making an impact?

- **The 30-Day Self-Audit:** Track what you do daily for a month. Are you learning new things, solving meaningful problems, or just repeating the same tasks?

- **No 'Start and End' in Mind:** Are you aimlessly working without a clear career goal? If you don't know where you're headed, you'll stay stuck.

- **The New Year's Resolution Loop:** Every year, you set ambitious career goals, only to end up doing the same things as last year. Sound familiar?

- **Colleagues are Advancing, and You're Not:** The junior developer you mentored last year? They're now leading a project, while you're still in the same role.

Funny Industry Reality: "The Senior Engineer Syndrome" You know that one engineer who's been at the company for 10+ years, and their knowledge is so specialised that their code is a black hole?

Reality Check: If your entire job depends on outdated tech that no one else understands, you're not "highly valuable"—you're stuck.

Reflective Prompt

Think about your past month at work. Which tasks or situations made you feel most stuck, and why? What's one small step you could take today to challenge that stagnation?

Identifying stagnation is step one, but breaking free often requires insights you can't see on your own. This is where mentors become invaluable—they help uncover blind spots and guide you toward solutions.

3. How Mentors Help Uncover Blind Spots

Ever spent hours debugging a cryptic issue, only for a colleague to spot the problem instantly? That's what mentors do for your career—they see what you can't. Mentors not only provide insights but also guide collaborative growth, encouraging you to learn and solve challenges together. Teamwork with mentors can uncover blind spots you may never have seen alone.

Reflective Prompt

Think about the last piece of constructive feedback you received. Did you act on it? If not, how could you revisit and apply it today?

Now that we understand the value of mentorship, it's time to translate that knowledge into actionable steps. Let's dive into a structured plan to debug your career and get back on the growth path.

4. The 30-Day Career Upgrade Plan—Unlocking Your True Potential Through Mentoring and Collaboration

Stuck careers aren't fixed by luck—they're fixed by design. With small, consistent actions over the next 30 days, you can move from stagnation to acceleration. This step-by-step approach focuses on diagnosing your career bottlenecks, leveraging mentorship, and collaborating with peers and industry leaders to achieve meaningful growth.

Week 1: Diagnose the Bottleneck—Find What's Holding You Back

The first step to any meaningful upgrade is figuring out where the problem lies. Whether it's outdated skills, a lack of visibility, or something else entirely, diagnosing the bottleneck is crucial.

Steps to Take

- **Run a Career Audit:** Take a critical look at your current role and responsibilities. Ask yourself:

  - Are you stuck in maintenance mode, repeating the same tasks every day without learning?

  - Are your current responsibilities aligned with your long-term career goals?

- **Get External Feedback:** Seek insights from trusted mentors, colleagues, or managers. Ask open-ended questions like:

  - *"What's one skill you think I should focus on improving?"*

  - *"How can I contribute to the team in a more impactful way?"*

- **Identify Your 'Technical Debt':** Just like in software development, technical debt accumulates when issues go unaddressed. In your career, neglected skills or delayed projects can pile up and eventually hold you back. *For example, that one legacy codebase no one wants to touch often mirrors the skills or challenges we've ignored, but addressing them can lead to surprising breakthroughs.*

- **Reflect on Emotional Barriers:** Examine self-imposed roadblocks such as fear of failure, hesitation to seek help, or reluctance to embrace new challenges.

Challenge: Ask a trusted mentor or peer: *"What's one thing I should do differently to grow?"*

Reflection and Transition to Week 2: "By identifying your bottlenecks, you've uncovered the areas holding you back. Now that you've diagnosed the problem, it's time to take focused action and start installing upgrades that move you forward."

Week 2: Install an Upgrade—Expand Your Skills and Network

Once you know what's holding you back, it's time to take action. Installing an "upgrade" means learning new skills and building a supportive network.

Steps to Take

- **Learn a New Skill:** Find a course, webinar, or workshop that excites you and aligns with your growth goals. Commit to completing it and applying what you've learned.

- **Collaborate on Projects:** Join team initiatives, participate in open-source development, or start a side project with peers. Collaborative projects help you build both technical and interpersonal skills. *Collaborating with peers and mentors not only expands your skills but also builds lasting connections that support your success.*

- **Refactor Your Network:** Reach out to mentors, industry peers, or influencers who inspire you. Engage in conversations to learn from their experiences and perspectives.

- **Work with a Mentor:** Share your growth goals with your mentor. Ask for specific advice on steps you can take to develop in areas where you feel stuck.

Challenge: Take one actionable step this week—enrol in a course, contribute to an open-source project, write a blog post, or connect with someone you admire professionally.

Reflection and Transition to Week 3: "With your upgraded skills and expanding network, you're starting to build momentum. Next, it's time to ensure that your efforts are seen and recognised by the right people to unlock more opportunities."

Week 3: Improve Visibility—Be Seen, Heard, and Valued

You've started to gain momentum—now it's time to ensure your efforts are noticed by the right people in your organisation and beyond.

Steps to Take

- **Build Your Brand:** Post insights, learnings, or achievements on platforms like LinkedIn, GitHub, or Medium. Regularly sharing your work and ideas can increase your visibility and credibility. For example, one software engineer consistently shared quick tips and coding insights on LinkedIn. Within a few months, their posts began attracting attention from industry leaders, leading to invitations to panel discussions and collaborations.

- **Volunteer for High-Profile Tasks:** Step up to lead or contribute to a project that demonstrates your skills and initiative. Even small leadership opportunities matter.

- **Engage with Communities:** Attend an industry meetup, join a panel discussion, or participate in online forums. Professional communities are excellent spaces for learning and networking. For example, after actively participating in local tech meetups, one developer connected with a startup founder and was invited to collaborate on an innovative project, expanding both their technical expertise and professional network.

- **Elevate Your Role Through Mentorship:** Start mentoring a junior colleague or someone new in your field. Teaching others not only solidifies your knowledge but also highlights you as a leader in your organisation.

Challenge: Commit to three visibility-boosting actions this week:

1. Comment on three posts from industry leaders.

2. Share one personal insight or achievement on LinkedIn.

3. Reach out to two professionals you'd like to connect with or learn from.

Reflection and Transition to Week 4: "Visibility builds credibility, paving the way for new opportunities to grow and lead as you enter Week 4. Now it's time to consolidate your progress and ensure sustained momentum."

Week 4: Final Testing—Deploy and Monitor Career Growth

The final week focuses on consolidating your progress and creating systems to maintain your momentum.

Steps to Take

- **Analyse Your Metrics:** Reflect on your actions over the past three weeks. Ask yourself:

  - What has improved as a result of my efforts?

  - What still needs more focus and work? Track progress on learning new skills, improving visibility, and building relationships. Quantify these if possible—like the number of posts shared, people reached out to, or challenges tackled. For example, note how many meaningful professional conversations you initiated or how you applied new skills to deliver impactful results.

- **Involve Your Mentor for Objective Feedback:** Schedule a check-in with your mentor to review your progress. A mentor can offer an unbiased perspective on your growth, point out areas you might have overlooked, and ensure you stay accountable to your goals. For instance, they can help refine your next steps, adjust your roadmap as needed, and keep you focused on sustainable progress.

- **Outline a 90-Day Roadmap:** Based on your progress, set clear, achievable goals for the next three months. Break them into smaller, actionable steps and add them to your calendar to ensure consistency.

- **Schedule Career Maintenance:** Regular career maintenance is vital for sustained growth. Plan quarterly check-ins with yourself and your mentor to reassess and realign your objectives. This habit ensures you're continuously evolving and addressing new opportunities or challenges as they arise.

- **Celebrate Milestones:** Recognise your successes, no matter how big or small. Acknowledging these wins reinforces positive habits and keeps you motivated. Share your achievements with your mentor, peers, or team as a way to inspire and connect with others.

💡 **Challenge:** Schedule a quarterly career check-in with yourself and at least one mentor to maintain your upward trajectory and adjust your goals as needed.

Reflective Wrap-Up Prompt: Use the next 30 days to take small, focused steps that lead to meaningful results. Write down:

- One skill you want to learn.

- One person you want to connect with.

- One way you'll contribute to your team or professional community.

Final Thought: Debug Early, Upgrade Often

"Your career isn't a static codebase—it's a dynamic system that thrives on learning, adaptation, and collaboration. Debug early, upgrade often!"

Chapter 7

Soft Skills, Hard Impact—Why Empathy and Communication Matter

Introduction: The Missing Piece in IT

Technical skills might land you the job, but it's your soft skills that determine how far you go. Many IT professionals focus intensely on improving their coding, debugging, and problem-solving abilities—but they underestimate the power of communication, emotional intelligence, and empathy.

The truth? A brilliant idea poorly communicated is as good as no idea at all.

Whether you're leading a team, working with clients, or collaborating across functions, your ability to connect, articulate, and empathise will directly impact your success.

Why Emotional Intelligence is an IT Superpower

What is Emotional Intelligence (EQ)?

Emotional Intelligence (EQ) is the ability to recognise, understand, and manage both your own emotions and the emotions of others. In the fast-paced, high-pressure world of IT, EQ is often the difference between effective collaboration and constant conflict.

Fight or Flight: How IT Professionals React Under Pressure

Picture this: You're in a critical discussion about a product launch, and things start getting heated. Someone challenges your idea. You immediately feel defensive.

At that moment, your brain triggers a fight-or-flight response.

- **Fight:** You argue back aggressively, dismissing their viewpoint. The discussion turns into a battle of egos rather than a productive debate.

- **Flight:** You shut down, stop contributing, and mentally disengage, missing an opportunity to influence the discussion.

Neither reaction is helpful. Emotional intelligence allows you to pause, process, and respond rather than react. Instead of arguing or retreating, you stay calm, ask clarifying questions, and guide the discussion toward solutions.

Sound familiar? We've all been there—it's like hitting CTRL+ALT+DEL on your emotions.

Practical Steps to Build EQ in IT

1. **Pause and Breathe:** The moment you feel defensive, take a deep breath before speaking. Use this pause to reset your thoughts and avoid reacting impulsively.

2. **Acknowledge Emotions:** Privately name the emotions you're feeling—e.g., frustration, fear, or irritation. Naming emotions reduces their intensity and helps you regain control.

3. **Shift to Curiosity:** Replace assumptions with questions like:

    - *"What's driving this person's perspective?"*

    - *"How can I clarify or adapt my idea to address their concerns?"*

Exercise: Role-Play Activity

Bring these steps into practice by role-playing a high-pressure conversation with a colleague or friend. • Take turns being the "challenger" and the "defender." • As the "defender," practice pausing, acknowledging emotions (e.g., "I feel frustrated"), and responding with curiosity rather than defensiveness. Ask clarifying questions like:

- *"Can you explain why you feel that way?"*

- *"What alternative approach would you suggest?"*

    - Reflect afterwards: Did you follow the steps effectively? How did staying composed and curious change the tone of the discussion?

Reflection Prompt: Think about a recent high-pressure conversation. How did you react? If you had used these steps and practised through role-play, what might you have done differently to apply emotional intelligence in that situation?

The IT Leader's Secret: Self-Regulation

Highly successful IT professionals and leaders—like Satya Nadella and Jeff Bezos—are known for their composure under pressure. They don't let emotions hijack their decision-making. Instead, they:

- Take a breath before responding.

- Listen actively instead of formulating their response while others are speaking.

- Ask thoughtful questions rather than making assumptions.
- De-escalate tension by acknowledging the other person's perspective.

Exercise: The next time you're in a challenging discussion, practice active listening by repeating back what the other person said before responding. Use phrases like, *"If I understand you correctly, you're suggesting..."* or *"Let me clarify..."*

Mastering emotional intelligence helps you manage difficult situations, but what about everyday interactions? Even in the most routine discussions, poor communication can create unnecessary confusion. Let's explore how communication gaps impact IT professionals and how to prevent them.

The Hidden Danger of Poor Communication

Soft skills aren't just about handling conflicts—they're also about ensuring clarity in the first place.

A Real-Life Story: When Communication Fails

I once explained a high-level concept to a colleague and even provided a detailed document to refer to later. During the discussion, they nodded along, seemingly understanding everything.

A few days later, they asked others for the same information, as if I had never explained anything. It wasn't a memory issue. Instead, they were simply avoiding reading the document and looking for an easier way out.

Why This Happens

1. Some people prefer quick answers instead of reading through resources.

2. Others avoid responsibility by pretending they were never given the information.

3. In some cases, it's a sign that communication wasn't effective.

How to Prevent This

- **Summarise Key Takeaways:** At the end of conversations, summarise the main points and confirm understanding.
  - Example: *"Just to recap, the three main points are... Does this align with your understanding?"*
- **Ask for Reflection:** Encourage the other person to rephrase or repeat key points.
  - Example: *"Can you summarise what we discussed to make sure we're on the same page?"*
- **Follow Up in Writing:** Send a follow-up email or message highlighting key details.
  - Example: *"As discussed, here's the document for reference. Let me know if you have any questions!"*

Exercise: Practice closing discussions with a simple recap: *"Before we wrap up, let's make sure we're aligned. The next steps are..."*

Communication isn't just about preventing misunderstandings—it's also a crucial skill for leadership. The best leaders aren't just the most knowledgeable; they're the ones who can guide and inspire others. Let's see how mentorship naturally cultivates leadership skills.

How Mentorship Teaches Leadership and Empathy

Mentorship isn't just about guiding others—it's about learning how to lead with empathy, patience, and clarity. Some of the best leaders in IT didn't start as natural-born managers; they honed their leadership skills through mentorship and collaboration.

From Mentor to Leader: Why Teaching is the Best Way to Learn

Many aspiring leaders think they need to be promoted to a formal leadership role before they can start developing leadership skills. This is a mistake. The best way to build leadership capabilities is through mentoring others—whether it's onboarding a junior developer, guiding a peer through a challenge, or even answering a colleague's technical questions.

Why Mentoring Develops Leadership Skills

1. **Active Listening** – Understanding where the other person is struggling before offering advice.

2. **Patience and Adaptability** – Explaining the same concept in different ways based on the mentee's learning style.

3. **Empathy in Action** – Recognising the challenges others face and offering guidance that aligns with their perspective.

4. **The Art of Giving Constructive Feedback** – Learning how to correct mistakes without discouraging growth.

5. **Building Trust and Influence** – Gaining respect by genuinely investing in someone's development.

Reflection Prompt: Who in your team or professional circle could benefit from mentorship? How could mentoring them help you grow as a leader?

Just as mentors need to develop empathy for their mentees, mentees also need to recognise the pressures their mentors face. Let's explore why mentorship is a two-way street.

Understanding Your Mentor's Perspective: A Two-Way Empathy Shift

Mentorship isn't just about what the mentor teaches the mentee—it's also about what the mentee learns about the mentor.

When the Mentor is Under Pressure

As a mentee, it's easy to feel frustrated when your mentor doesn't give you a clear answer or seems too busy to explain things in detail. But before assuming that they're ignoring you, take a step back and understand their situation.

- If they seem stressed or distracted, they might not be able to give you their full attention at that moment.

- If your question isn't urgent, wait for a better time to ask.

- Acknowledge their situation. A simple, *"I see you're busy— I'll check in later,"* shows empathy and builds a stronger relationship.

Reflection Prompt: Think about a time when you felt frustrated with a mentor or leader. What could you have done differently to show empathy and strengthen that relationship?

Industry Insight

How Jeff Bezos and Satya Nadella Built Influence Through Storytelling and Communication

Jeff Bezos: The Power of Storytelling

At Amazon, Bezos banned PowerPoint presentations in executive meetings. Instead, he required six-page narrative memos that tell a compelling story. Why? Because people remember stories, not bullet points.

Lesson: If you want to persuade and influence in IT, focus on clear, structured communication that tells a story.

Satya Nadella: Leading with Empathy

When Nadella took over as Microsoft's CEO, he focused on culture and communication. He transformed Microsoft by listening to employees, fostering collaboration, and emphasising empathy in leadership.

Lesson: Success in IT isn't just about intelligence—it's about connecting with others, understanding their needs, and inspiring them toward a shared vision.

Steve Jobs – The Art of Persuasion

Jobs was famous for presenting new ideas with conviction. Instead of just showing data, he told a compelling story, turning product launches into must-watch events. His storytelling ability made Apple products more than just technology; they became part of a lifestyle.

Lesson: This makes the "Soft Skills = Influence" argument even stronger.

Key Takeaways

- **Build emotional intelligence** to effectively navigate conflict and foster collaboration.

- **Enhance communication** to ensure clarity and prevent misunderstandings.

- **Mentor others** to grow your leadership skills and inspire your team.

- **Practice empathy** by understanding the challenges others face, including mentors, peers, and colleagues.

- **Influence through storytelling, empathy, and clear communication** to drive impactful change in IT.

Remember, the most impactful IT professionals aren't just masters of code—they're masters of connection.

Chapter 8

The Power of Reverse Mentorship—Learning from Juniors and Peers

Why Even CTOs Learn from Junior Developers

Fun Fact: The world's youngest self-made billionaire in tech? Mark Zuckerberg, who built Facebook as a college student. If his seniors had ignored him, social media as we know it might not exist today!

Tech Moves Fast—And So Should Learning

Senior leaders may have deep industry experience, but junior developers are often the first to experiment with new technologies. AI, blockchain, and modern frameworks are evolving so rapidly that today's fresh graduates often bring hands-on expertise with cutting-edge tools.

Lesson: Great ideas don't care about experience levels—they care about execution.

Case Study: Mark Zuckerberg & Facebook's Early Engineers

When Facebook was built, Zuckerberg's team of young engineers in their early 20s disrupted the tech industry.

- Senior tech leaders dismissed social networking as a niche idea.

- Zuckerberg and his team proved otherwise, transforming how the world connects.

Lesson: Ignoring junior perspectives can mean missing the next big tech revolution.

It's not just tech entrepreneurs who prove the value of reverse mentorship—even managers and senior developers can gain tremendous insights by embracing junior perspectives.

Not Just CTOs—Managers Should Learn from Juniors Too!

Fun Fact: At just 18 years old, Erik Finman became a Bitcoin millionaire by investing $1,000 in cryptocurrency at age 12. He later launched education-focused startups, proving how young innovators disrupt industries and inspire even seasoned professionals.

Senior managers often shift their focus from hands-on coding to team management, deadlines, and business strategy. However, staying connected to junior developers ensures they:

- Stay updated on evolving coding trends.

- Make better-informed technical decisions.

- Build stronger team relationships and trust.

Lesson: If tech giants learn from young disruptors like Erik Finman, senior leaders should listen to junior developers.

Common Barriers to Reverse Mentorship
What Holds Senior Leaders Back?

- *"Why should I learn from someone younger?"*

- Fear of looking inexperienced.

- The false belief that *"Experience > New Knowledge."*

It's easy to think, *"What can I possibly learn from someone who still asks me how to configure their IDE?"* But the answer might surprise you. Younger developers often bring fresh perspectives, hands-on knowledge of emerging technologies, and ideas you might not have considered.

How to Overcome These Barriers

- Shift from ego to curiosity → Ask, *"What can I learn from their perspective?"*

- Normalise mentorship exchanges between juniors and seniors.

- Focus on collaboration, not hierarchy.

Example: At Google, senior engineers attend workshops led by junior developers on AI, ML, and new programming paradigms to stay ahead in the field.

While overcoming these barriers requires a mindset shift, fostering a culture of shared learning takes deliberate action. Here are some proven strategies to make it happen.

How to Foster Shared Learning in Tech Teams

Fun Fact: The first version of Linux was built by a 21-year-old student, Linus Torvalds. Today, Linux powers over 90% of cloud servers and supercomputers worldwide!

The best engineering teams thrive when knowledge flows both ways. Here's how to create a culture of shared learning:

- **Pair Programming** – Let juniors write code while seniors review and guide them. Often, juniors surprise seniors with fresh techniques and insights!

- **Cross-Team Hackathons** – Pair juniors and seniors to build real-world solutions.

- **Lunch & Learn Sessions** – Let juniors lead sessions on trending technologies.

- **Tech Blog Contributions** – Encourage juniors to write about emerging trends, while seniors refine and validate the ideas.

- **Role Reversal Days** – Have juniors guide seniors through hands-on training in AI, cloud, and automation tools.

Lesson: Never underestimate a fresh perspective. The next Linus Torvalds might already be on your team.

This approach not only keeps teams technically updated but also strengthens trust, team cohesion, and overall innovation.

Case Study: When a Junior Developer Mentored a Senior Leader in AI

Scenario: A senior software architect at a Fortune 500 company had 15 years of experience in software engineering but minimal exposure to AI.

- A junior developer, who had recently completed a deep learning certification, stepped in.

- The junior introduced machine learning automation, helping the senior optimise workflow efficiency by 40%.

- The senior, in turn, used their expertise in system architecture to transform the junior's idea into a scalable application.

Expanded Insight: The senior's guidance ensured the AI-powered workflow seamlessly integrated into the company's larger ecosystem. By combining the junior's AI knowledge with the senior's system-level expertise, they achieved a balance between innovation and real-world scalability.

Fun Fact: Some of the biggest AI breakthroughs came from interns at Openai and Google. A 19-year-old AI intern helped develop a reinforcement learning model that revolutionised robotic automation!

Lesson: Help juniors, and they'll help you back. Reverse mentorship is a two-way street.

The Shift Toward Reverse Mentorship in Tech Culture

Many top companies now embrace reverse mentorship as part of their culture.

- **Google's 20% Time Policy** → Employees (junior & senior) collaborate on passion projects.

- **Airbnb's Data Science Culture** → Senior executives rely on junior data scientists to guide business decisions.

- **Tesla & Spacex** → Musk's brightest engineers are young, proving impact > seniority.

Lesson: The most successful tech companies don't just teach juniors—they learn from them.

Key Takeaways

- **Leverage junior developers' expertise** to stay ahead of tech trends.

- **Break hierarchical barriers** to foster shared learning and collaboration.

- **Encourage reverse mentorship exchanges** to drive team innovation and trust.

- **Recognise that learning isn't about seniority—it's about relevance.**

Remember, the most successful tech professionals don't lead from above—they collaborate to learn and grow with their teams.

Final Thought: "Reverse mentorship isn't just about bridging generational gaps—it's about harnessing diverse expertise to solve today's fast-paced challenges. Learning isn't hierarchical—collaboration drives innovation."

Engage in Reverse Mentorship: Practical Exercise

To put the principles of reverse mentorship into practice, try this exercise:

1. **Identify a Junior Colleague**: Choose someone whose skills or experience you admire. Think about what they've recently mastered—whether it's AI, a new programming language, or a modern framework.

2. **Schedule a Knowledge-Sharing Session**: Set aside 30 minutes for a one-on-one session where they can teach you about their expertise or demonstrate a tool they've worked with.

3. **Reflect on the Insights**: After the session, jot down what you learned. Ask yourself:

    - How can I apply this knowledge in my role or team?

    - What further questions can I explore to deepen my understanding?

4. **Share the Experience**: Share your appreciation for their insights, and consider how you can continue collaborating for mutual growth.

Outcome: This exercise not only enriches your technical knowledge but also builds trust and fosters collaboration between you and the junior colleague.

Key Takeaway: *Learning isn't about seniority—it's about staying relevant.*

Part 3

Thriving Through Mentorship and Collaboration

From Coder to Leader—Your Mentorship & Growth Roadmap

Introduction: Why Leadership Isn't Just for Managers

Leadership doesn't begin with titles—it starts with actions. Before diving into the steps to develop leadership qualities, let's explore why taking initiative now, without waiting for formal recognition, matters.

Surprising Fact: Did you know that over 60% of first-time managers struggle in leadership roles because they were never prepared for it? The reality is, leadership doesn't start with a title—it starts with actions.

Many IT professionals wait for a title before stepping into leadership, but leadership is a mindset, not a promotion. The real shift happens when you start:

- Guiding others

- Mentoring colleagues

- Influencing without authority, and most importantly…

- Building meaningful connections that unlock your true potential.

This chapter will break down a structured roadmap to help you go from an individual contributor to a leader, whether or not you have an official title yet.

Creating Your Board of Mentors

Success isn't achieved alone—it's nurtured through the support and wisdom of mentors. But how do you build this essential network? By identifying key mentorship roles, you can ensure comprehensive growth.

Why You Need Multiple Mentors

One mentor can't provide all the answers. You need different perspectives for different aspects of growth:

* **Technical Mentor** – Keeps you sharp in your domain.

* **Career Mentor** – Guides your long-term career strategy.

* **Leadership Mentor** – Helps you build influence and people skills.

* **Peer Mentor** – Provides real-time support and accountability.

Don't Underestimate Reverse Mentorship

Often, mentorship isn't just top-down—it's two-way. As we explored in the previous chapter, even senior leaders benefit from reverse mentorship, where junior developers introduce them to new technologies, AI tools, and industry trends. This mutual exchange of knowledge strengthens both mentees and mentors.

Real Story: The "Board of Mentors" Approach—How One Engineer Built a Leadership Pipeline

Scenario: A mid-level engineer named Daniel felt stuck in his career. His technical skills were strong, but he wasn't getting noticed for leadership roles.

Instead of waiting, he proactively built a "Personal Board of Mentors":

- **Technical Mentor** – A principal engineer who helped him deepen his expertise.

- **Career Mentor** – A senior manager who guided him on career strategy.

- **Leadership Mentor** – A VP who taught him how to influence and lead teams.

- **Peer & Reverse Mentors** – A junior developer who introduced him to AI and automation trends.

Highlighting Mutual Learning: The reverse mentorship with the junior developer didn't just boost Daniel's technical knowledge—it showcased his openness to learning and adapting. By embracing fresh perspectives, Daniel demonstrated the mindset of a growth-oriented leader.

What Happened?

- Within a year, Daniel had improved both his leadership and visibility.

- When a leadership role opened, he was the first choice.

- His mentorship board continued guiding him, even as he became a leader.

Takeaway: Success isn't a solo journey. A structured mentorship approach accelerates growth, and learning from junior developers can give you a competitive edge.

How to Find and Approach Mentors Through Networking

Once you've mapped out the types of mentors you need, the next step is to actively connect with them. This is where strategic networking comes into play—not just reaching out but engaging meaningfully with industry leaders, colleagues, and peers.

Knowing that you need mentors is one thing—finding them is another. The best way to connect with the right mentors isn't by cold messaging strangers—it's by networking the right way.

Tap into Existing Networks

Your next mentor could be closer than you think. Leverage:

- **Your Workplace** – Senior colleagues, managers, or cross-functional leaders can offer informal mentorship. Start by asking for advice on a small challenge.

- **Industry Events & Meetups** – Conferences, hackathons, and tech summits are goldmines for connecting with experienced professionals. Don't just attend—engage in discussions!

- **Online Communities** – LinkedIn, Twitter, and Slack groups allow direct access to industry leaders. Engage with their posts, ask insightful questions, and build relationships.

The Mentorship-Driven Networking Mindset

Too many people approach networking as "What can I get?" Instead, shift to "What can I contribute?"

- Offer insights, share knowledge, and support others—this builds credibility.

- Help others connect—become a connector, and people will want to connect with you.

If You Struggle to Find a Mentor…

Start by mentoring someone else. Teaching accelerates learning, and mentorship is a two-way street—helping others attracts mentors to you.

Take Action: Identify one person you could reach out to for guidance, or someone you could mentor!

Mentorship isn't just about finding the right mentors—it's also about becoming one when the opportunity arises.

Step 1: Start Small—You Don't Need a Title to Mentor

While learning from mentors is crucial, you shouldn't wait to start contributing yourself. Mentorship is a two-way street, and guiding others is a powerful way to develop leadership skills in any role.

You might think mentorship is reserved for senior engineers or managers, but the truth is, mentorship starts with small acts of guidance:

- Helping a junior developer debug an issue.

- Reviewing a peer's code and providing constructive feedback.

- Sharing a career lesson with someone who's facing a challenge you've already tackled.

Step 2: Identify Who You Can Mentor

You don't have to wait for an official mentorship program. Look for:

- A junior developer who needs guidance.

- A peer who wants to improve a skill you've mastered.

- Someone outside your team (e.g., a mentee in a tech community).

Step 3: Make It Intentional—Set a Simple Goal

After identifying people to mentor, it's important to focus your guidance on achievable and impactful goals. This intentional approach strengthens your mentoring relationships and prepares you for larger leadership opportunities. Good mentorship isn't just casual advice; it's **focused guidance**.

- Help a mentee learn a new skill (e.g., system design, public speaking).

- Offer career navigation support (e.g., switching domains, handling promotions).

- Share insights on leadership (e.g., influencing without authority).

Leadership often begins when you mentor others, without even realising it

Mentoring others is a key pillar of leadership, but equally important is how you communicate and inspire action. This is where storytelling comes into play.

The Power of Storytelling in Leadership & Mentorship

As you step into mentorship and leadership roles, communication becomes essential, and storytelling is your key to inspiring and connecting with others. Let's see why this skill can transform your impact, both technically and as a leader. Facts inform, but stories inspire. The best IT leaders don't just explain ideas—they tell stories that:

- Make technical concepts relatable

- Inspire teams with a vision

- Motivate mentees to push through challenges

Real Story: The "Soft Skill" That Got an Engineer Promoted

Scenario: Priya, a senior developer, was frustrated. She had great technical ideas but struggled to get buy-in from leadership.

One day, her mentor advised her to start using storytelling in meetings. Instead of diving into raw data, she framed her solutions as narratives.

Example: Instead of saying,

"This algorithm reduces processing time by 30%."

She said,

"Right now, every time a customer places an order, they wait 5 extra seconds. Imagine removing that wait time—every user instantly feels the difference. This algorithm cuts that delay, improving user experience and retention."

What Happened?

- Leadership started listening to her ideas.

- She became the go-to engineer for high-impact projects.

- Within six months, she was promoted to Engineering Manager.

Takeaway: The best technical solutions don't always win—the best-communicated solutions do.

Leadership Spotlight

Satya Nadella—How Storytelling Transformed Microsoft

Now that we understand the power of storytelling in technical roles, let's look at how it influences larger organisational changes. Satya Nadella's transformation of Microsoft demonstrates how stories drive innovation and empathy in leadership.

When Satya Nadella took over as Microsoft's CEO in 2014, the company was struggling with internal silos and a rigid culture. Rather than simply issuing new corporate strategies, Nadella used storytelling to drive change.

- He told the story of his connection to empathy—how raising a son with special needs taught him to listen, understand, and adapt.

- He framed Microsoft's transformation as a shift from a "know-it-all" culture to a "learn-it-all" culture."

- Instead of just presenting business metrics, he shared real stories of employees and customers, making Microsoft's mission feel personal and relatable.

What Happened?

- Microsoft shifted to a growth mindset culture.

- Employee engagement and innovation skyrocketed.

- The company's market value more than tripled.

Takeaway: Great leaders don't just give instructions—they inspire action through storytelling. Whether you're leading a small team or an entire company, stories connect people to a vision.

Storytelling Exercise

Turn Technical Solutions into Inspiring Stories

Think about a technical challenge you've solved recently. Instead of presenting it as raw data or results, frame it as a compelling story:

1. **Identify the Problem**: What was the issue, and who was affected by it?

2. **Describe Your Solution**: How did you approach the challenge, and why was your method impactful?

3. **Emphasise the Outcome**: Highlight how your solution made a difference—did it save time, improve user experience, or solve a critical bottleneck?

💡 *Practice Sharing*: Share this story with a colleague or in your next team meeting. Observe how framing the solution as a narrative changes the way your audience engages with your ideas.

These examples show how everyday actions—mentorship, empathy, and storytelling—can shape effective leadership. Whether it's onboarding a colleague or addressing team morale, leadership starts with small, intentional steps.

1. The First-Time Mentor: How an Engineer Became a Leader Without Realising It

Scenario: Alex, a software developer, was asked by their manager to onboard a new junior colleague. At first, Alex saw it as just another task, focusing on showing the new hire the ropes.

What Happened? By guiding the junior developer, Alex realised they were not just sharing knowledge but also shaping a new team member's growth. Through the process, they built confidence, developed empathy, and started improving their communication skills. When a team lead role opened, their mentoring experience was cited as a key reason for their promotion.

Takeaway: Leadership often begins with simple acts of guidance and sharing. You don't always need a formal title to influence others and grow as a leader.

2. Leadership Through Empathy: A Story of Crisis

Scenario: During a high-pressure sprint, a mid-level manager noticed a team member struggling with burnout. Instead of pushing harder for results, the manager scheduled a one-on-one conversation to understand the issue.

What Happened? The team member opened up about personal challenges, and the manager adjusted workloads while offering additional support. This act of empathy created trust and loyalty, improving team morale and long-term productivity.

Takeaway: Leadership isn't about always being the hero—it's about showing understanding and prioritising the well-being of your team.

The ACT Framework in Action: Ask, Connect, Thrive

The ACT Framework ties together everything we've explored in this book—from mentorship to networking and leadership. It's the foundation for building relationships and taking ownership of your growth.

Throughout this book, we've explored mentorship, networking, and leadership. If you look closer, all these concepts follow a simple three-step process: **Ask, Connect, and Thrive**. This isn't something new—ancient wisdom has emphasised these principles for centuries. Now, let's break it down into an actionable framework.

Your **career is in your hands**—you're in charge of your success.

☑ **Ask** – The right questions to the right mentors.

☑ **Connect** – Build meaningful professional relationships.

☑ **Thrive** – Take action, grow, and step into leadership.

As you step into leadership through the **Thrive** phase, storytelling becomes a powerful tool to inspire and connect with your team. Leadership isn't just about execution—it's about inspiring others to action. By transforming data and technical concepts into relatable stories, you can motivate your team, gain buy-in for your ideas, and align everyone toward a shared vision.

Real Story: How ACT Transformed a Career

Rahul's journey illustrates the power of applying ACT principles to real-life scenarios. His career transition highlights how each step—asking, connecting, and thriving—unlocks opportunities and confidence for growth.

Scenario: Rahul, a backend engineer, felt his career was plateauing. He wanted to move into technical leadership but didn't know where to start.

What Happened? He applied the ACT Framework

☑ **Ask:** He reached out to his manager and asked for growth opportunities.

☑ **Connect:** He built relationships with senior engineers and tech leads.

☑ **Thrive:** Rahul didn't just focus on delivering tasks—he used storytelling during team meetings to explain how his solutions impacted the company's goals. This inspired his colleagues and earned him recognition as a leader.

Outcome

- Within a year, Rahul became a tech lead.
- His confidence and leadership skills skyrocketed.
- The ACT approach helped him accelerate his career growth.

Takeaway: The best career shifts happen when you **ask, connect, and take action.**

ACT Framework Reflection Exercise

To put the ACT Framework into action, take a few minutes to reflect on the following:

1. **Ask**: Write down one actionable question you'll ask this week. For example:

   "What skills do you think I should prioritise to grow in my role?"

2. **Connect**: Identify one person you'll build a meaningful professional connection with—whether it's a mentor, colleague, or someone in your broader network.

3. **Thrive**: Choose one leadership task to step into this week. This could be mentoring a junior, leading a discussion in your next team meeting, or proposing a process improvement.

Pro Tip: Block time on your calendar to complete these actions so they don't get lost in the shuffle.

The Continuous Learning & Leadership Roadmap

Once you've implemented the ACT Framework to kickstart your career growth, the next phase is maintaining momentum.

Continuous learning keeps leaders relevant and adaptable in today's rapidly evolving industry.

Leadership isn't a one-time achievement—it's a lifelong journey. Even the best leaders keep learning and adapting to stay relevant.

Key Areas to Focus On

- **Technical Depth** – Stay updated with emerging technologies in your domain.

- **Communication & Influence** – Master storytelling, public speaking, and persuasion.

- **Decision-Making** – Learn to make clear, confident choices under uncertainty.

- **Emotional Intelligence** – Keep developing self-awareness, empathy, and resilience.

How to Keep Learning

Leadership isn't static—it requires ongoing development across technical, emotional, and interpersonal skills. Let's explore practical methods to integrate continuous learning into your career roadmap.

- **Books & Courses** – Read leadership books, take online courses on LinkedIn Learning, Coursera, or Udemy.

- **Shadowing Leaders** – Observe how great leaders handle meetings, decision-making, and mentoring.

- **Real-World Learning** – Join cross-functional projects to gain experience beyond your current role.

Final Exercise: Create Your 6-Month Leadership Growth Plan

Now that you have the tools to foster growth, it's time to create a personalised plan. This exercise helps you set measurable goals and actionable steps to ensure consistent development.

Take **5 minutes** to outline:

1. **What leadership skill will you focus on first?** (Communication, decision-making, mentoring?)

2. **Which learning method will you use?** (Book, course, mentorship?)

3. **What's your measurable goal?** (e.g., "I will lead a tech talk in my company within 3 months.")

Takeaway: Leadership isn't just about what you know—it's about how you keep learning

Key Takeaways

The principles we've covered—mentorship, storytelling, and the ACT Framework—are interwoven into leadership success. As you progress, keep these lessons at the forefront of your journey.

- **Step into leadership before the title**— influence and guide others through mentorship and collaboration

- **Build a personal board of mentors** to accelerate your growth and gain diverse perspectives.

- **Harness the power of storytelling** to make technical solutions and leadership ideas resonate powerfully with your audience.

- **Embrace reverse mentorship** to learn from junior colleagues and stay ahead in emerging technologies.

- **Follow the ACT Framework (Ask, Connect, Thrive)** to take charge of your career and unlock leadership opportunities.

Challenge for Readers: Write down one mentor you will reach out to this week. If you don't have one yet, start by sharing your knowledge with a peer—mentorship is a two-way street.

Final Thought

Start now. Take ACTion. Your career is in your hands. **Ask, Connect, Thrive—because leadership isn't given, it's built.**

Chapter 10

Ancient Wisdom for Careers—How ACT Has Always Driven Growth

Wisdom That Stands the Test of Time

The challenges we face in IT today—career stagnation, self-doubt, and the need for strong networks—aren't new. They've existed for centuries, and history offers profound lessons on how to navigate them.

Ancient wisdom repeatedly reinforces a simple truth: **No one succeeds alone.** From mythology to modern leadership, the most transformative career shifts happen when we:

- **Ask** for help in times of doubt.
- **Connect** with the right mentors and peers.
- **Thrive** by leveraging collective wisdom.

This is not a new concept—it's a timeless strategy. Whether it was Arjuna seeking Krishna's counsel, Hanuman realising his true power through Jambavan, or Rama forming alliances with Sugriva, history has shown that progress is built on guidance, collaboration, and support.

In this chapter, we'll explore how the **ACT Framework** (Ask, Connect, Thrive) is not just a modern career strategy but a principle deeply rooted in ancient wisdom.

Arjuna & Krishna: The Power of Asking for Guidance

The Moment of Doubt That Changed Everything. Arjuna stood on the battlefield, frozen, not because he lacked skill, but because doubt clouded his mind. He questioned his abilities, his purpose, and the decisions he had to make.

But Arjuna did something crucial: he asked for help. He turned to Krishna, his mentor, for clarity. Through Krishna's guidance, he gained the perspective needed to move forward with confidence.

Modern Insight: Asking for Help at Crucial Moments Many IT professionals experience an Arjuna moment—a time of uncertainty where self-doubt makes decisions feel impossible.

- Should I switch careers or stick with my current path?

- Am I ready for leadership, or should I remain an individual contributor?

- Should I invest time in learning a new technology?

In IT, asking the right questions at the right time can unlock opportunities—whether it's feedback during code reviews, clarity on career goals, or advice on emerging industry trends. Professionals who embrace mentorship gain the perspective and confidence needed to overcome doubt and move forward.

The most successful professionals don't have all the answers—but they know whom to ask. Like Arjuna, they seek mentors, managers, or peers who provide clarity and direction.

Key Takeaway: Asking for guidance isn't a weakness—it's a strategic advantage.

While Arjuna's story highlights the importance of seeking guidance in moments of doubt, Hanuman's journey shows us how the right connections can help unlock potential we didn't even realise we had. Both stories emphasise that growth often requires external support and encouragement—whether it's a mentor, a peer, or someone who sees what we cannot.

Hanuman & Jambavan: Unlocking Hidden Potential Through Connection

The Strength That Was Always There Hanuman possessed incredible strength, but at a crucial moment, he forgot his power. When the Vanara army needed someone to cross the ocean, he hesitated—until Jambavan reminded him of his capabilities. That realisation changed everything, and Hanuman leapt that no one else could.

Modern Insight: Finding Mentors Who See What You Cannot. Many IT professionals underestimate their skills:

- Hesitating to apply for a senior role, believing they're not "ready."

- Thinking public speaking, mentoring, or leadership isn't for them, until someone pushes them to try.

- Struggling with imposter syndrome, questioning whether they belong in the industry at all.

A mentor, like Jambavan, sees potential before it's realised, offering encouragement that enables professionals to stretch their limits and achieve breakthroughs. Just as Jambavan reminded Hanuman of his power, IT leaders often help their teams discover strengths they didn't know they had.

Key Takeaway: Sometimes, you don't need new skills—you need someone to remind you of what you already have.

Hanuman's self-discovery demonstrates the value of mentorship and individual realisation. In contrast, Rama's alliance with Sugriva reveals the importance of collaboration and building networks for collective success. Together, they show that thriving often depends on both internal breakthroughs and external alliances.

Rama & Sugriva: Thriving Through Alliances

Why No One Wins Alone. Rama didn't defeat Ravana by himself. He allied with Sugriva, built a trusted army, and won through collaboration. This underscores a fundamental truth: Success is never a solo journey.

Modern Insight: Building Strong Professional Networks. Too often, professionals believe hard work alone is enough. But in reality:

- The best career opportunities come through connections, not applications.

- The most successful leaders don't just know things—they know people.

- The greatest innovations come from teams, not individuals.

Whether through mentorship programs, cross-functional teams, or professional networks like LinkedIn, IT professionals thrive by forming alliances that accelerate opportunities and create lasting impact. Collaborative efforts—just like Rama's alliance with Sugriva—prove that the best outcomes come from collective strength.

Key Takeaway: Your network is your net worth. Strong alliances aren't optional—they're essential.

"These stories of seeking guidance, unlocking potential, and thriving through collaboration form a timeless blueprint for success. They remind us that the challenges we face today are not new—they echo the struggles and triumphs of those who came before us. The ACT Framework takes these enduring principles and translates them into actionable steps, giving you a clear path to apply them in your IT career."

ACT Framework: The Timeless Formula for Career Success

The Ask, Connect, Thrive (ACT) Framework isn't a new concept. It has existed throughout history in different forms, proving one thing:

Those who seek guidance, build strong networks, and collaborate effectively are the ones who succeed.

How to Apply Ancient Wisdom in Your IT Career

1. **ASK like Arjuna**—Seek mentors and guidance in moments of doubt.
2. **CONNECT like Hanuman**—Find those who recognise and amplify your strengths.
3. **THRIVE like Rama**—Build alliances and grow through collaboration.

Whether in ancient battlefields or modern boardrooms, these principles remain timeless and powerful.

Final Thought

Success isn't just about what you know—it's about whom you learn from, whom you trust, and whom you build with.

The ACT Framework has existed for centuries. It's time to use it to accelerate your career. 🚀

Closing Words

The ACT Framework has always existed, guiding leaders from ancient battlefields to modern IT careers. Success isn't just about what you know—it's about whom you learn from, connect with, and grow alongside. Go forward with the courage to ask, the wisdom to connect, and the generosity to thrive. **Ask. Connect. Thrive.**

Conclusion:
Ask, Connect, Thrive—Unlock Your True Potential and accelerate your career

Your journey toward success begins now

Picture this: It's a year from today, and you've taken charge of your growth. You've reached out to mentors who've guided you through challenges, built genuine connections that opened doors, and taken bold steps to become the leader you've always envisioned.

It all started here—with one choice, one action, one decision to invest in yourself.

Success Isn't a Solo Journey

Every great career story has a turning point—one Ask that changed everything, one Connection that unlocked unexpected opportunities, one moment of courage that set someone on the path to Thriving in the IT industry.

This book has been about unlocking your true potential through mentorship, meaningful relationships, and bold action.

Now, it's your turn.

Recap: The Ask, Connect, Thrive (ACT) Framework

Every successful IT leader follows three simple, yet transformative principles:

ASK—Your Growth Begins With a Question

- ✔ Every career transformation starts with a simple ask—for guidance, mentorship, or feedback.
- ✔ Overcome hesitation and ask the right questions—specific, thoughtful, and actionable.
- ✔ **Remember:** *Google can't give you a promotion, but a mentor can.*

CONNECT—The Right Relationships Unlock Opportunities

- ✔ Your network is your net worth—stop collecting contacts and build real, trusted relationships.
- ✔ Move beyond traditional networking—give before you ask and build a circle of meaningful connections.
- ✔ Mentorship is a two-way street—learn from juniors, peers, and senior leaders.

THRIVE—Turn Knowledge into Action

- ✔ Leadership doesn't start with a title—it starts with impact.
- ✔ Apply storytelling, emotional intelligence, and mentorship to grow from a coder to a leader.
- ✔ Career success isn't about working harder alone; it's about working smarter with the right people.

The ACT Framework doesn't just accelerate your career—it also prepares you to lead with impact, influence, and empathy. As you ask for guidance and build meaningful connections, you'll discover the leader within you.

Ancient Wisdom Meets Modern Growth

The ACT framework isn't new—it's ancient wisdom applied in a modern context. From Arjuna seeking Krishna's guidance to Rama relying on Hanuman, history has shown that seeking help is a strength, not a weakness. The greatest leaders have always known when to ask for help, whom to connect with, and how to thrive through collaboration.

Your success story follows the same timeless path.

What's Next? Take Action Today!

Reading this book is just the beginning. **Your growth depends on what you do next.**

- **Ask for guidance**—Identify one person you admire and reach out for advice or mentorship. Use the Perfect Ask Template to craft your message.

- **Build real connections**—Engage in a meaningful conversation with a colleague, mentor, or industry peer. The Networking Cheat Sheet can help you start.

- **Thrive through contribution**—Mentor someone, share knowledge, or step into a leadership role. Begin with the 30-Day Growth Plan to structure your journey.

Challenge: *Take one action today—send that message, schedule that call, offer help, or seek advice. One step can change everything.*

Resources & Exercises

To help you put these lessons into action, here are tools to guide your mentorship and career growth:

- **The "Perfect Ask" Template** – A proven script for reaching out to mentors, managers, and industry leaders.

- **The Networking Cheat Sheet** – Practical strategies to build relationships that lead to real opportunities.

- **30-Day Growth Plan** – A step-by-step roadmap to mastering mentorship, leadership, and storytelling.

- **Personal Board of Mentors Worksheet** – A guide to identifying and tracking the mentors you need for career success.

Get access to these at [YourWebsiteHere].com or join our mentorship and networking community.

Final Thought: Your Future Starts Now

Imagine the career you want to build, the people you'll impact, and the legacy you'll leave behind

Every great IT career is built on three things:

☑ A bold **Ask**

☑ A strong **Connection**

☑ And the courage to **Thrive**

"The impact you create today will ripple through your team, your organisation, and your industry. Be bold, be generous, and be the leader you were always meant to be."

This book has given you the tools—but **only you** can take the first step.

What will you do today to Ask, Connect, and Thrive?

Tag or message a mentor who has helped you. Then, pay it forward—be the mentor you once needed.

Let's connect! Share your biggest takeaway from this book and how you'll apply it.

Your success story starts now. Go build it. 🚀

References for Index

1. https://www.legends.report/steve-jobs-mentor-who-was-bill-campbell/

2. https://www.inc.com/carmine-gallo/the-trillion-dollar-coach-who-mentored-steve-jobs-google-guys-showed-them-a-simple-powerful-communication-tactic.html

3. https://cio.techgig.com/technology-unplugged/teachers-day-who-are-the-mentors-of-mark-zuckerberg-bill-gates-and-richard-branson/articleshow_b2b/85900410.cms

4. https://www.gatesnotes.com/25-Years-of-Learning-and-Laughter

5. https://www.factualamerica.com/decoding-elon/musks-mentors-key-figures-in-elons-journey

6. https://economictimes.indiatimes.com/magazines/panache/teachers-day-special-paying-tribute-to-mentors-of-jeff-bezos-elon-musk-mark-zuckerberg/whats-life-without-a-mentor/slideshow/85897346.cms

7. Mentoring Statistics in 2024 [https://www.mentoringcomplete.com/mentoring-statistics-everything-you-need-to-know-in-2024/]

8. 19 Workplace Mentoring Statistics[https://www.soocial.com/workplace-mentoring-statistics/]

9. 40+ Definitive Mentorship Statistics[https://www.mentorcliq.com/blog/mentoring-stats]

10. LinkedIn Workplace Learning Report[https://learning.linkedin.com/resources/workplace-learning-report]

11. Top Online Mentoring Platforms[https://igotanoffer.com/en/advice/best-mentoring-platforms]

12. https://www.brandvm.com/post/20-youngest-self-made-billionaires

13. https://www.inc.com/business-insider/when-billionaires-made-their-first-million.html

14. https://www.brandvm.com/post/20-youngest-self-made-billionaires

15. https://www.investopedia.com/news/who-erik-finman-bitcoin-millionaire-teenager/

16. https://en.wikipedia.org/wiki/Linus_Torvalds

17. https://history-computer.com/people/linus-benedict-torvalds-creator-of-linux-operating-system/

18. https://www.cnbc.com/2021/12/16/google-20-percent-rule-shows-exactly-how-much-time-you-should-spend-learning-new-skills.html

19. https://www.dataversity.net/case-study-an-inside-look-at-airbnbs-data-science-journey/

20. https://deltabase.io/culture-head-to-head-series-working-for-elon-musk/

21. https://www.factualamerica.com/decoding-elon/musks-mentors-key-figures-in-elons-journey